BLUEBACKS

How to Vet, Buy, and Run a Profitable Blue-Collar Small Business

TRIPP PARKER

The information provided in this book is for informational purposes only and is not intended to be a source of advice or investment analysis with respect to the material presented. The information and/or documents contained in this book do not constitute legal or financial advice and should never be used without first consulting with a qualified professional to determine what may be best for your individual needs.

The publisher and the author do not make any guarantee or other promise as to any results that may be obtained from using the content of this book. You should never make any investment decision without first consulting with your own qualified professionals and conducting your own research and due diligence. To the maximum extent permitted by law, the publisher and the author disclaim any and all liability in the event any information, commentary, analysis, opinions, advice and/or recommendations contained in this book prove to be inaccurate, incomplete or unreliable, or result in any investment or other losses.

Content contained or made available through this book is not intended to and does not constitute legal advice or investment advice and no attorney-client relationship is formed. The publisher and the author are providing this book and its contents on an "as is" basis. Your use of the information in this book is at your own risk.

Names: Parker, Tripp, author.

Title: Bluebacks : how to vet, buy, and run a profitable blue-collar small business / Tripp Parker.

Description: Fort Mill, South Carolina : Tricar Holdings LLC, [2026] | Includes bibliographical references.

Identifiers: ISBN: 9798996482900 (hardcover) | 9798996482917 (softcover) | 9798996482924 (ebook) | 9798996482931 (audiobook)

Subjects: LCSH: Small business--Ownership. | Entrepreneurship. | Blue collar workers.

Classification: LCC: HD2341 .P37 2026 | DDC: 338.642--dc23

I dedicate this book to my sons, Teddy and Liam, who will inherit this, God willing.

TABLE OF CONTENTS

INTRODUCTION: A NEW PLAN

You know that old feminist cliché? Which one, you ask? Yeah, I know, there are plenty. But I mean this one in particular:

> Well-behaved women rarely make history.

We men have our own now, and it goes like this:

> Well-behaved men rarely make money.

You know how it goes . . . A good, kind, respectful, strapping young Christian man wants to succeed in life. So he follows the responsible path. He plays the odds and takes the safe route. He's all about the adult thing to do. The guy studies hard, works harder, and tries hardest. The idea is to follow the great American script—credential, career, climb, cabanas (enjoyed daily poolside in retirement somewhere warm). A man tries to do everything right. He honors his elders, obeys his parents, and impresses his pastor. See, this way of work is presented as virtuous—be stable, be safe, don't take unwise risks, don't get too distracted, don't get "weird" and chase pipe-dream fantasies. From church, this guy hears the same message but wrapped in spiritual language—be a provider, don't be slothful, love God not money, humble yourself, pay your dues, be nice and respectful to all women and perhaps a middlingly attractive one will marry you.

He does everything right and gets absolutely wrecked. That whole world is completely gone. The cost of pretending otherwise is not theoretical anymore. It's showing up in debt, anxiety, stagnation, layoffs, and a growing sense of betrayal—especially among men who did what they were told, the way they were told, and are now being punished for it. Men have been lied to about university, the job market, and "success." Not only lied to by secular institutions but often lied to inside organizations that claim to care about truth—our churches. And young men aren't the only ones dealing with the consequences. I see three groups colliding into the same wall at the same time—three generations, three sets of pressures, one unavoidable question:

> If the old plan doesn't work anymore, what does a real plan look like now?

Let's start with our **young** kings and their lot in life. More and more of them can tell college is a scam. They can feel it in the pricing, the debt, the cultural contempt, and the downstream reality—a degree that costs a fortune and increasingly delivers less than promised. They're told they need university to have a future, but then they graduate with a pile of debt and a job market that can't absorb them. One quarter of all unemployed Americans have a college degree.[1]

On top of that, many are told—explicitly or implicitly—that they're the problem. That they should sit down, shut up, and be grateful for whatever scraps they're given. The message becomes, *You took on debt, you played by the rules, now accept the penalty for being who you are—an irredeemable straight white Christian male.*

You might have seen the mega-viral *Compact Magazine* article by Jacob Savage entitled "The Lost Generation." A key excerpt:

> The doors seemed to close everywhere and all at once. In 2011, the year I moved to Los Angeles, white men were 48 percent

---

1 Polymarket (@Polymarket), "JUST IN: Americans with college degrees now make up a record 25% of all unemployed," X (formerly Twitter), November 24, 2025, https://x.com/polymarket/status/1992959480213213669.

> of lower-level TV writers; by 2024, they accounted for just 11.9 percent. *The Atlantic*'s editorial staff went from 53 percent male and 89 percent white in 2013 to 36 percent male and 66 percent white in 2024. White men fell from 39 percent of tenure-track positions in the humanities at Harvard in 2014 to 18 percent in 2023.
>
> In retrospect, 2014 was the hinge, the year DEI became institutionalized across American life.
>
> In industry after industry, gatekeepers promised extra consideration to anyone who wasn't a white man—and then provided just that. "With every announcement of promotions, there was a desire to put extra emphasis on gender [or race]," a former management consultant recalled. "And when you don't fall into those groups, that message gets louder and louder, and gains more and more emphasis. On the one hand, you want to celebrate people who have been at a disadvantage. On the other hand, you look and you say, wow, the world is not rooting for you—in fact, it's deliberately rooting against you."[2]

Of course guys of a certain persuasion want out of that system. Who wouldn't want to go their own way for being openly, consistently discriminated against *despite* having more education, experience, and accolades?

Great. OK. Freedom. Right. Now what? Exactly. Younger men don't all know how to opt out in a rational, measured way, and one that actually offers a better future. They aren't being shown viable alternatives with clarity and seriousness. They're being offered cryptocurrencies and gambling (but I repeat myself).

---

2 Jacob Savage, "The Lost Generation," *Compact,* December 15, 2025, https://www.compactmag.com/article/the-lost-generation/

When we combine the debt load with the diminishing payoff, what becomes obvious is that the primary education to university to corporate job pipeline is a doomed one for a growing number of men.

Meanwhile, **mid-career** men are already feeling that gloom. These guys followed the old script and have lived it for years, maybe one and a half to two decades-plus now. This guy's got one helluva résumé. He built real experience. He might even have prestige, status, clout. But he's watching wages stagnate, watching layoffs hit teams that were once considered safe, watching the nature of his work become more fragile by the year. He isn't sure his job will be around in twenty years. He's not sure it will be around in five. Or less.

This particular gentleman has deep experience inside corporate systems—meetings, processes, deliverables, performance reviews—and he may not know what he would do outside that environment if the job ends. Uncertainty springs anxiety, the kind you can't solve with a motivational podcast about being your own boss-entrepreneur-CEO or whatever.

Despite the headstart, your middle-aged middle-manager types are worse off than their younger brothers, cousins, and nephews. A lot of these men are married. Many have kids. Some have a mortgage. A decent net worth on paper. Keyword, *paper*. Their entire lifestyle is about as fragile.

There's a broader labor-market reality that even mainstream outlets have been reporting, which is that white-collar workers are increasingly "spooked" by AI and the layoffs that mass adoption triggers.[3] Many feel their security slipping away, because it is. In five years (or less), what businesses *won't* be replaced or made obsolete by AI?

---

3 Rachel Louise Ensign, "Spooked by AI and Layoffs, White-Collar Workers See Their Security Slip Away," *Wall Street Journal,* December 16, 2025, https://www.wsj.com/economy/jobs/white-collar-workers-job-anxiety-d8f83885.

If you don't plan now, you're in for a world of hurt. But as with the younger guys, what kind of plan? Every month, there's a new "get-rich-quick and escape corporate scam" lie. Many fall for it and buy whatever internet marketing video course the guru-of-the-month is selling. Many more *would* fall for it if the deception weren't so obvious.

Now, both generations may have a bone to pick with their dads and uncles. We're talking about the **boomer** demographic. Business owners, specifically, who started back when the old script rang true and played out fairly. These guys had the skills, put them to use, and built something real and tangible. Before personal brands, there were real businesses. That's what these guys built: real businesses that fed their families, employed people, served customers, and kept working even when the economy changed then changed again and changed back then changed some more.

But many of these owners have no—and here's that word again—*plan* for their future. They have a business, but no heirs to take it over. It may be too small for private equity to care about. It produces income, but it isn't positioned for an easy, clean sale. It's more a job that they own than anything. You can't sell a salary. Michael Gerber spent forty years trying to teach small business owners that they're not entrepreneurs; they're "technicians"—people who are experts at doing the work, not owning and running a business that trains and hires people to do said work (Gerber called this "The E-Myth"). And so they reach the edge of retirement and realize they're stuck between bad options. They want something to walk away with other than a small stipend and great, big tax bill. They're worried that's the best-case outcome. Their worst-case fear is that they'll have to close shop and retire with nothing while their employees get stranded and their customers lose a provider they've relied on for years.

The baby boomer business blow-up isn't some niche, rare circumstance. From *Business Insider*:

> Across the US, older business owners are arriving at the same juncture. Over half of small businesses — those with a single owner and fewer than 500 employees — are owned by people over 50. The wealth-management firm NewEdge Wealth has estimated that boomer-owned businesses in the US are worth about $10 trillion. Those boomers can't retire and enjoy their sunset years until they figure out what to do with their businesses. Can a relative or longtime employee take over? Should they shut down? Or can they sell? For millennials with the entrepreneurial bug, this boomer retirement bomb could be a boon.[4]

Do you see it now?

You do.

Multiple generations. **Different** problems. **One solution**.

We have young men trying to avoid debt slavery but lacking a clear alternative. Then we have mid-career white-collar men watching their security erode and realizing their skillset may be trapped inside a shrinking category. And we have boomer owners holding real businesses that need succession and not abandonment.

Multiple problems across multiple generations, but there is one practical solution that can connect them. I know because I lived it.

---

4 Ann C. Logue, "The Great Boomer Fire Sale," *Business Insider,* October 1, 2024, https://www.businessinsider.com/boomers-selling-small-businesses-investment-opportunity-millennials-gen-z-retirement-2024-10.

WHAT HAPPENED TO ME

I graduated with highest honors from Duke University in 2007 with a triple major—Electrical and Computer Engineering, Computer Science, and Philosophy. I then spent more than fifteen years working for some of the most prestigious employers in tech—Microsoft, Amazon, and others.

I worked on artificial intelligence and machine learning applications in multiple contexts, including ad targeting for search ads, healthcare initiatives like vocal biomarkers and heart rate algorithms, and fraud detection in banking. I managed a team with a research and development budget of over $260 million.

In 2022, I became convinced that I was, in effect, automating away my own job. Not just my specific role, but the broader category of white-collar knowledge work I had built my career around. So I began looking for an exit plan—something real—before that door narrowed.

I also became convinced about that same time that there were going to be fewer and fewer of these jobs going forward, and that straight white Christian men in particular would be first on the chopping block as promotions increasingly flowed to minorities and women.

Then in 2023, I was laid off. I was explicitly told it was *not* due to job performance. I noticed something. Zero white men survived the layoffs in my group. I said nothing of it, got my severance pay, and started the search for a new job.

Prior to that sudden layoff, I had never failed to get a job I interviewed for. This time, it took me six months—and a severe pay cut—to land another role despite what I consider nearly unmatched credentials and references. Then again, I hadn't interviewed for a new job that I had needed since prior to 2014. Isn't that interesting.

Underemployment hardened my hunch into certainty—good-paying white-collar jobs like the ones I'd had since college graduation were (and are) going away, and if you don't build an alternative, you are volunteering to be trapped inside a shrinking market where you get less and less juice from a tighter and tighter squeeze.

So I began the move from corporate tech to what I call a **white-collar, dirty-job entrepreneur**. Mix the collars and you get what's also called **gray collar**. Or more familiarly, **blue collar**.

OWN WHAT CAN'T BE AUTOMATED

My solution is simple to state and hard to do but worth it all anyway. If you're a young man thinking about going to university, and doing that specifically for career prospects . . . maybe don't do that. Go into a grayish-blue-collar gig that has future promise, like electrical, HVAC, plumbing, and other work that is not going to be automated. This does not mean you have to do field work forever. But you do need to learn it. Then learn how to manage it. Then learn how to manage the business. And eventually, own the business.

And if you're like I was—a mid-career corporate professional—you need to plan an exit. That looks like lining up financing the way you would if you were buying a house. You get preapproval then begin a business search to vet companies that can not only pay you, but also build wealth, careful *not* to buy one that's basically an E-Myth job where you're paying for an asset only to get . . . ass.

Now, I need to be careful . . . I am *not* promising that you can put up a website and print money. Not at all. I am promising something far more grounded—that you can find a business to own, run, and build into something that can make more money than you ever made in corporate. If you do it correctly.

I'll show you. That's what I wrote this book for. I will show you real-world examples of how to do it and what to look for. I will provide real examples of industries with promise for the young men and the mid-career men. I will provide real examples of businesses I've vetted over the past several years, ones I liked but didn't get due to price or other issues, ones I didn't like, ones that were con jobs, and ones that were good and I bought.

And if you're a boomer seller, my instruction is going to be urgent. Start searching for men in those first two camps now. Find ways to structure the deal so you get a fair price—not a fire sale. Make it easier for a buyer to take the business off your shoulders and pay you what it's worth over time, with a transition period. Don't wait until the last second. If you do, you may walk away with nothing. Your business may be stripped for parts. Your employees may be left in the cold.

This can be a win-win-win for every generation, but only if you undergo the business buying-selling adventure intelligently. I'll show you how, with real-world examples of how to structure deals so the seller gets a fair price without crippling the business with too much debt to service (a deal that "wins" on paper but breaks the business in real life is not a win for anyone long term).

By the time you finish this book, you will understand:

- How you've been lied to—and taught to think about work, university, and "success" in a way that's not only financially ruinous, but in many cases not biblical.
- How the future of the economy is actually going to work, and how to plan for it and take advantage of the transition.
- How to approach and evaluate small and medium-sized businesses to take advantage of what is shaping up to be the largest wealth transfer in the history of mankind. In other words, the lies you were told can work to your

benefit . . . if you play it right.

Practically speaking now, you will learn how to:

- Accurately price a business and recognize its strengths and weaknesses. This is more than looking at tax returns. It's about knowing what you're looking at when you receive a small business P&L and balance sheet so you can tell a bad deal from a good one—and knowing who to bring in as a third party so you don't make a catastrophic mistake.
- Find deals—both lots of deals and the best deals.
- Understand what brokers mean when they say "SDE" or "Adjusted EBITDA," what those terms should mean, and what you must ask to confirm they mean what they should.
- Bring in financing if you don't have all the cash.
- Know who writes the contract, and who vets the financials.
- Know what to learn about key employees, whether you have what it takes to run the business, and what you must do so that post-close you're not living inside a disaster.
- Be creative with deal structure, including the levers you can pull beyond purchase price.
- Make it a win-win for you and the seller because the levers go well beyond the number on the top line, and because the best deals are often created, not found.

Good, smart Christian men in America need a new plan to earn a living, provide for a family, and leave a lasting community legacy.

This is that plan.

CHAPTER 1

Real Motivation, Real Business, Real Money

I'M GOING TO SAY SOMETHING UP FRONT THAT will annoy the part of you that wants certainty before action, which is natural human psychology.

> If you wait until you feel "ready," you will stay exactly where you are.

See, the old script has us play to ask for permission and look for guardrails. We're led to believe that the responsible man is the one who avoids risk. And that's true—right up until the day the system decides you're the risk because you're a straight white Christian man and you get laid off.

With this book I am giving you more than a plan, I'm offering a perspective shift. We will move you from having been a human resource within someone else's machine, to on a reasonable timeline owning a machine yourself. That requires something more than interest. You will need to burn some ships. There are no half measures in ownership. If you approach this like a side hobby you dabble in when you have leftover energy, you'll either never close a deal—or you'll close a bad one out of impatience and confusion. Either way, you'll "prove" to yourself it doesn't work, and you'll retreat back to the familiar. Enjoy that underemployment. Barista with a master's degree. Same energy.

Like Michael Gerber taught, business-owning is different from business-working. Ownership is not permission-based; it's performance-based. Following this book, you'll be trading a life where your future is decided in rooms you're not in, for a life where your future is decided by the quality of your decisions and the value you create by them.

That trade scares a lot of people. It should. It's heavy. But it's also how to get your dignity back. You can't get canned for being the "wrong" demographic if you're the one in the position to do the canning.

MOTIVATION THAT WORKS: 3 Reasons You Can't Forget When It Gets Hard

This is the part of the book where I give you the anti-get-rich-quick-scheme. It's more like *how-to-own-an-asset-the-hard-way-but-because-it's-hard-fewer-people-will-do-it-and-for-that-reason-alone-you-have-a-built-in-advantage*.

For most men, the drive to **win** in business ownership shows up in three ways:

- economic
- technological
- theological (if you're a person of faith)

Economic: You Don't Build Wealth by Being Hired

A paycheck can feed a family, pay a mortgage, and partially fund a retirement account. But it is not the same thing as **wealth**. Wealth is what remains when you stop working. The fastest way most ordinary men build real wealth is *not* by squeezing a few extra percentage points out of a 401(k). It's by acquiring a cash-flowing asset, then improving it.

Ownership is the only way to make your effort compound. See, as an employee, effort is linear. *Work hard; get paid. Stop; it stops.* But as an owner, effort can become **structural**. You build systems, you build teams, you build retention, you build recurring revenue. The business can keep producing even when you're not personally pushing every button. You own something that produces cash because the market needs it.

Your wealth is now tied to boring value creation that doesn't go out of style and can't be gambled away, rug-pulled, and lost to the latest influencer's social media marketing course.

Technological: You Need a Business That Lives in Reality

If your plan relies on moving "bits"—pure digital work—then you're staking your future on the most compressible category of labor on earth. Every digital business can be copied, automated, bundled, or outsourced (there's that "AI" again).

This is why I became obsessed with a simple mantra when I was sick and tired of underemployment: **atoms, not bits.**

Atoms are the physical world. Atoms break. They wear out. They leak, and they fail. Atoms require maintenance and require replacement. And so real-world problems keep demanding real-world solutions. That's what I decided I want to own—companies that solve the problems that remain stubbornly physical. A software-only company is fragile for the average man who wants stability and control. To paraphrase Michael Gerber, who always said to "work on your business, not in it," I say "make software be in your business; don't make software your business."[5]

I wanted a company where the value delivery can't be completed by sending an email. I wanted the kind of company where the work is done by people who show up, touch the world, and fix what is broken. Where trenches get dug, utilities get installed, pipe and wire get laid, equipment gets serviced, buildings get built, and businesses get valuation for doing all of the above. Assets not jobs.

Theological: If You Believe in Stewardship, This Is Not Optional

If you're a person of faith, you know your "why" so to speak—why business ownership could be worth your while, even if it takes months to years, not hours to days.

As a Christian, I believe provision is responsibility and stewardship is obligation. I believe a man should not build his children's future on a structure that depends on permission from institutions that can change the rules overnight to target you, specifically, for holding these exact beliefs.

Ownership is a **stewardship** vehicle. It's a way to create resilience, dependable provision, and the ability to be generous and durable in a volatile world. And for a man trying to live faithfully, "safe" is not the same thing as "wise." Sometimes "safe" is just another word for "dependent." Yes, this or that internet business may

---

5 Ilene Frahm, "Work ON It, Not Just IN It," Inside EMyth, accessed May 28, 2026, https://www.emyth.com/inside/work-on-the-business-not-in-the-business.

seem lower risk and higher reward, but it's a castle made of e-sand. What's here today is gone tomorrow. If it's as easy as opening up a digital storefront and selling the same product anyone else can, anyone else will. The easier the ride, the more broken-down and beat-up the vehicle. I don't make the rules.

A real-world, gray- or blue-collar business, in contrast, has demand that persists, customers that return, a service that actually matters, and operations that can function beyond one heroic person. It has systems and standards and a way of producing quality at scale. It's also got a moat—maybe not a sexy moat, but a real one, made up of licensing, specialized equipment, compliance, scheduling complexity, long-standing customer relationships, local reputation, workforce management, and operational know-how.

And you can just show up and **buy** such a business.

OK, now THAT sounds too easy. If anyone could do it, anyone would.

That's what some of you are thinking right now. Fair enough. There are serious questions you have that make sense to address before we get to the how-to.

I'm an abrupt kind of guy, so let's abruptly pause the lesson here. Let's address your fears, uncertainties, and doubts about buying and growing a physical goods and services business to build a new career right now.

CHAPTER 2

It Can't Be That Easy

IF CHAPTER 1 WAS ABOUT MOTIVATION, AND IT WAS, this chapter is about what shrinks motivation into barely-flaccid wishes. That culprit is **suspicion**.

I recently got hit on Facebook with an advertisement for buying a mobile ice machine dispenser startup business. You know those giant freezers outside a lot of gas stations and inside some grocery stores that let you buy a giant bag of ice? In the American South, those are essential, not optional. It's hot. The week I wrote this chapter, half the country got dumped with more than a foot of snow. But down in the Deep South, there were areas it still felt like summertime. A perfect region for one of these mobile ice businesses, right?

Well, let's read the ad a little more closely. It obviously reads like it was written by an artificial intelligence app, but I want you to notice the bait-and-switch:

> Most people want a business in a box.
>
> Few have the capital, patience, and discipline to build it.
>
> [Trademarked business name] is for the few.
>
> One machine, $29K, no staff, no ads — just 35–45 bags/day = $3K–$4.5K/mo in real profit.

> Pays for itself in 7–10 months, then it prints.
>
> We handle the entire rollout.
>
> You just collect.

That's the bait; here's the switch, after you've read all that stuff which sounds too good to be true because it probably is:

> If you're looking for "cheap" or "easy," skip this.
>
> If you're ready to deploy smart capital into a real asset, CLICK BELOW to schedule a meeting with a real expert…
>
> Limited placements only.

What do you think? Do you think people really fall for that? Probably.

Imagine you're on the inside; imagine you're the ice machine startup salesperson. At just under thirty grand a pop, you can set up a virtually guaranteed-profitable asset. Are you really going to sell off all that cashflow? Or are you going to scrap together $3 million to buy a hundred of them and become a passive income millionaire?

Or are you going to advertise to the world that you've struck gold (ice in the hot South), and you're renting access to your proven mine for just about anyone to get while the getting is good?

It's laughable. Beyond that, there's the two tones of the ad. First, we're told how easy it is, ending in, "You just collect." To repurpose a viral meme created by President Donald Trump . . . *Wow . . . Really? Wow . . . You're telling me this for the first time*. Pardon our presidential incredulity. You tell us how hassle-free and hands-off this business opportunity is, then try to play keep-away and castigate us for wanting "cheap" and "easy" . . . which is what you told us your business is? Do people really fall for that?

Probably. This chapter's title is "It Can't Be That Easy" because it's not. Likely-scammy ice machine businesses aside, buying a (real) business is **easier**— relative to potentially decades of underemployment during which you have to put off your hopes and dreams and continually downgrade your lifestyle just to keep up with inevitable inflation. We've got to just keep our guard up because if you don't realize you're a mark for dark money, you will become one.

As much as I personally do believe in buying a business, there are real, legitimate objections to this alternative career path. Let's hit 'em now, starting with one that comes up right after reading about starting an ice machine business.

OBJECTION: "Isn't It Better, Faster, and Cheaper Just to Start My Own Business?"

This is the most common objection I hear, and it often comes from the startup crowd. It usually comes from guys who instinctively assume that buying a business is overpaying for something you could build yourself.

On paper, this objection sounds reasonable. Why go through months of broker conversations, NDAs, due diligence, financing, and a twelve-to-eighteen-month ownership transition . . . when you could just start the same thing yourself? Why buy someone else's plumbing business when you can just start your own plumbing business?

Well, that objection collapses the entire challenge into one word . . . "start."

People treat "starting" like a single action. Like launching a website. Or ordering business cards. Putting up a Google Business Profile. That sort of thing. But building a durable, profitable service business is not *start* work; it's **build** work. Building has a brutal phase most people underestimate.

Zero to One Is Harder than One to Ten

Going from zero to one is an entirely different kind of difficulty than scaling from one to ten.

When you buy a business, you're buying a machine that's already producing output. Maybe imperfectly, maybe inefficiently, maybe with owner-dependence that needs to be replaced. But still, it's producing. It has customers. It has employees (or at least a labor model). It has operations, a reputation, and real momentum.

When you start from scratch, you don't get any of that. You get uncertainty, and you pay for that uncertainty in cash and time. If you're coming from a white-collar background—as most of my target readers are—then you also carry a specific handicap. You may have the entrepreneurial drive. You may have the managerial mindset. But you usually do not have the technical skill. That gap matters.

A simple way to understand this is the classic breakdown from *The E-Myth*:

- The *entrepreneur* sees opportunity and takes risks.
- The *manager* builds systems and processes.
- The *technician* does the actual work.

If you're stepping into trades and services—electrical, HVAC, plumbing, trenching, utilities, specialty fabrication—you cannot ignore the technician component. If you start from scratch and you're not the technician, then what are your options? Well, you've got two:

1. You personally become the technician (which takes time and training), or
2. You hire technicians before you have customers.

Option two is what destroys new service businesses; you start paying people before revenue exists. You're burning cash before the flywheel is even moving. Which brings us to the second reality the "just start it" people usually gloss over.

Customers are everything.

Even if you had technical talent on day one, you still have the same problem every startup has. Revenue! How long will it take you to acquire enough customers to cover your costs? Will it take twelve months to break even? Eighteen? Twenty-four? And that's the best scenario, where you're decent at marketing, decent at sales, and you don't get crushed by the early chaos of operations.

Now do the math. If it takes you eighteen to twenty-four months to crawl to break-even, you didn't "save money." You merely shifted the payment into time, stress, and risk. You may end up spending the same amount you would have spent buying an existing business, except you spent it to create something fragile.

And if the startup fails, you don't have a sellable asset. You have equipment, maybe. But not a customer list with retention. Not receivables. Not a working team. Not the infrastructure of something proven. Not good.

So, buying a business is not paying for something you could build. It's paying to skip the most dangerous phase, the phase where you bleed money and still don't know if the market will accept you.

"But startups are how people get rich, really rich," some may say at this point. Fair enough. In software, that logic historically worked because software had one giant compensating advantage—scale. A software company can scale to the entire planet. That was the bet.

Now, contrast blue- and gray-collar businesses. A plumber in one geography does not scale to 8 billion people. So you don't get to play the same venture math. No investor is going to hand you cheap millions with no personal guarantee so you can "build market share" in Toledo. And even if they did, you'd still be stuck with the same constraints of labor, schedules, and other mainstays of physical reality.

That's why, for most non-wealthy founders, starting from scratch in these categories is often more risky, not less.

You can lose money for years with limited upside, or you can buy something that is already making money, then structure the deal so you're protected while you learn.

Which leads to the next objection that tends to hit right after the first.

OBJECTION: "Doesn't It Take the Same Money to Break Even as It Does to Buy?"

In many cases, yes. In plenty of cases, it's more. At a startup, you're paying for time to build reputation, time to acquire customers, time to recruit and keep technicians, time to learn mistakes the market punishes, and time to find operational stability. That's a lot of time. And that time is not free because it is not paid as hours and minutes; it's paid in cash burned, opportunities cost (and lost), and stresses mounted.

By contrast, when you buy the right existing business, do your due diligence correctly, and model cash flow realistically, you're not bleeding for years hoping you'll eventually arrive at profit. You are paying debt service while you are already operating in profit. Maybe not at the "post-debt" level yet—but you're not living in a multi-year loss desert.

It's a different psychological experience, too. Most people don't appreciate how much "bleeding cash" changes your decision-making. When you're losing money each month, your brain starts sprinting toward desperate moves—cheap hires, cheap marketing, cutting corners, underpricing, chasing bad customers, taking any work you can get. That's not grit; that's panic. Buying a real business isn't easy, but it is often a way to avoid panic-mode entrepreneurship.

OBJECTION: "But These Businesses Are Personal-Goodwill Businesses. The Owner Leaves, and the Business Collapses."

This is one of the most intelligent objections, and it's where a lot of people, frankly, get scammed. The fears are simple, and they sound like so:

- "The customers are loyal to the owner."
- "The employees are loyal to the owner."
- "The relationships are personal."
- "When the owner sells and disappears, the whole thing falls apart."

Fear is real, which is why any serious acquisition strategy has to treat it as a first-order problem.

But you don't solve personal goodwill risk by pretending it doesn't exist. You solve it by structuring the deal so you're protected and designing the transition so you inherit the trust.

This is where the real estate analogy becomes useful. In a house purchase, you don't let the seller control the inspection. You don't let the seller pick the appraiser. The bank protects itself by lending only a percentage of value. That's not cynicism. That's how adults protect capital.

Buying a business must be treated the same way. Except the stakes are higher.

3 Protections That Serious Buyers Use

1. YOU ASSUME A REVENUE DROP AND MODEL IT HONESTLY.

You don't buy on "best case." You buy on, "What happens if 10 to 20 percent of revenue falls off because the owner fades?" If the business cannot survive a conservative drop, it's not a buy. Or it's a buy at a different price.

2. YOU REQUIRE A TRANSITION PERIOD.

The transition is not optional. It's how relationships transfer. You want the owner around long enough that customers and employees don't experience a jarring cliff. The owner fades. You rise. Quietly. Gradually. Intentionally. Rise and win.

3. YOU DON'T PAY ALL CASH.

This is non-negotiable if you want protection. A portion of the price is seller-financed over time, with interest. That creates alignment. If the seller gets 100 percent of the payday at closing and walks away, you have no leverage. But if the seller has money on the line for the next few years, the seller is incentivized to help the business succeed after the sale.

This isn't a "creative tactic." It's standard practice among intelligent buyers, like private equity, sophisticated operators, everyone. If a seller refuses seller notes and refuses protective structures, that refusal often tells you something. Usually, something unpleasant.

OBJECTION: "If I Ask for Seller Financing and Escrow, Won't I Lose the Deal to Someone Who Doesn't?"

Sometimes. And that's fine. If someone is willing to pay 100 percent cash at your valuation, don't compete with them. Walk away. That deal is not for you. Most legitimate deals do not work that way, because the exact problems we've been discussing are obvious to every serious buyer.

Sellers want the payday. That's normal. But sellers also have to accept reality—if the business truly depends on them, then the buyer must have protection against post-sale collapse. So the question is not "seller note or not."

The question is "how much seller note, how much escrow, and how structured is the transition." In practice, you communicate this early—often in the "Letter of Intent" stage. Not as an insult, but as a professional structure.

And if the seller has never sold a business before (which is common), part of your job is to educate them, e.g., "Here's why this protects us both . . . Here's why this is standard . . . "Here's why even institutional buyers do it . . ."

OBJECTION: "Dirty Deals. Scams. Hidden Payables. Fake Receivables. How do I avoid getting ripped off?"

This is where skepticism turns healthy. Because yes, dirty deals exist. This is a high-dollar transaction where many sellers are unsophisticated, emotionally attached, and sometimes willing to do shady things to maximize their payday. So you treat the purchase like adults treat a major purchase, and you build in protections. Here's how.

The Core Protection Stack

QUALITY OF EARNINGS

Pay a third party to validate what's real. Not due to paranoia but because you are not a fool.

WORKING CAPITAL AND RECEIVABLES/PAYABLES VALIDATION

You don't assume the books are clean. You confirm or deny. But don't skip this.

ESCROW HOLDBACK

This is the parachute if something is discovered after closing. I'll give you a practical example—sellers who early-bill customers right before closing to inflate receivables . . . while keeping invoices out of the system to artificially lower payables.

If you close with no holdback, you may end up holding the bag. If you have escrow, you can correct it.

Sellers who refuse basic protections often do so because protections prevent scams. Sure, some sellers will walk away the moment you insist on escrow or seller notes. Sometimes, that's a gift. It means you avoided a problem you would've discovered later at a much higher price.

OBJECTION: "Nobody Sells a Truly Profitable Business."

That statement gets repeated like a proverb. It's also false. People sell profitable assets all the time. They sell stocks that made them money. They sell real estate that has positive cash flow. They sell businesses that work. The real question is . . . why would a working business be for sale?

And there are more reasons than most people realize. The most common reason is simple: aging out with no successor. Picture the classic case. A boomer owner is mid sixties through seventies. The business works. It's worth real money. But the owner has no heir who wants it. He has daughters who chose different careers. He has a son who doesn't want the stress. He has no internal successor he trusts.

So what does he do? He sells.

But there's another reason boomer businessmen try to cash out instead of keep it.

Generation Bootstrap Psychology and the Non-Mentor Boomer

In a rational world, a business owner would identify a promising employee five to ten years out, mentor him, transition responsibilities, and eventually sell internally.

But many boomers did not do this. Some refuse to mentor. Some refuse to admit they had help. Some have pride. Some, shame. Some simply don't trust anyone enough to hand the keys over. They may care about their employees while still refusing to empower them. And that contradiction produces a very specific seller profile:

- high control
- low trust
- poor succession planning
- but a valuable, working business

These businesses don't have a natural institutional buyer if they're under a certain EBITDA threshold, and they don't have a natural internal buyer because the owner refuses to reveal the truth of the books. So they go to the market. If you understand the psychology, you can navigate the transaction far more intelligently.

Shame, Compensation, and Hiding the Books

One of the most important insights in your transcript is also one of the most uncomfortable. Many owners are embarrassed by how much they make relative to key employees who run most of the operation.

They may have a number-two guy who makes $160,000 and is effectively running the company . . . while the owner takes home millions. If that second-in-command ever sees the books, he will revolt. So the owner refuses to sell internally; that would threaten identity, pride, and perceived moral legitimacy. Be careful. That said, you're not private equity, so you don't trigger the "vulture" narrative. But you also aren't the employee who will feel personally betrayed. You're an outsider who can pay fair market value and allow the owner to exit without some kind of civil war.

OBJECTION: "What If I'm Not Buying a Business, I'm Buying the Owner's Two or Three Full-Time Jobs?"

This is the ghost-profit objection, and it's one of the biggest traps in small business acquisitions. Sometimes what looks like profit is actually the founder absorbing multiple roles for free:

- CEO
- sales
- operations
- customer support
- employee therapist
- quality control
- special relationship management

The business "profits" because the owner is doing work that would require hiring two to three people. If you buy that, and you replace the owner with paid labor, the profit vanishes. So you don't ignore this objection; price for it. You do the work of uncovering it. Ask:

- What does the owner do daily, weekly, monthly?

- What relationships are personal?
- What customer rituals exist that aren't on the books?
- What employee rituals exist that keep retention stable?
- What is truly required to maintain customer satisfaction?

Then, compute the true cost of replacement. If it requires hiring a COO, a GM, and a senior technician, you back those costs out and adjust valuation. This is how you avoid buying a job. Bring it back to that essential transition year; you want the owner behaving normally while you learn what's real.

OBJECTION: "What If the Seller's Customers Are All Boomer Businesses, Too? Isn't That a Race to the Bottom?"

What if your revenue as a brand-new business owner is actually tied to other aging businesses who are also going to disappear, sell, or collapse? It's a fair concern, and the correct response is not handwaving. The correct response is analysis.

Customer Concentration and Stability

Ask for the top customers and the percentage of revenue they represent. Then, research those customers. Like so:

- Who owns them?
- How stable are they?
- Are they national firms?
- Are they likely to outlive the boomer wave?
- Do they have institutional continuity?

If one customer represents an unhealthy share of revenue, treat the risk like an adult and adjust structure accordingly (more holdback, larger seller note, lower upfront, or you walk).

The counterpoint now is that competition is dying faster than demand. In many "atoms" industries, demand persists or rises . . . while competition collapses because owners age out and no successors exist. That means you may be walking into a market where the number of competent providers is shrinking.

That's not a race to the bottom. That's the opposite. The danger in these industries is not running out of work, it's running out of labor. In other words, the constraint is technicians, not demand. And that's a real issue, but it's a different issue than the "my customers will disappear" fear.

OBJECTION: "What About Illegal or Foreign Labor Comes in and Undercuts My Prices?"

This objection is real in certain markets and certain industries. But it's less a fatal objection and more a diligence requirement. If you're really concerned about this, keep this questions in mind:

- How many helpers, field techs, foremen, and supers exist?
- What is average tenure?
- What is average pay?
- Is the company underpaying relative to market?
- If so, what happens when you correct pay to retain talent?
- Does the margin structure support market wages?

If you discover the entire margin depends on underpaying, reprice the business, or you walk. If the company pays above market because it commands premium work and premium trust, you've got to validate that story. Are gross margins actually consistent with that premium positioning?

And remember . . . LOIs (letters of intent) are not promises. These are what you write and send to a business owner stating that you're a serious interested buyer, by the way. But that doesn't begin the sale; it begins the conversation. Now comes the due diligence. And if diligence reveals that a $3/hour wage correction is needed across the workforce, again, the price has to change, or you're out.

THE OBJECTION UNDERWRITING ALL OF THEM: "If Buying a Business Is So Wise, Why Aren't More People Doing It?"

There's a difference between a correct path and an effortless path. Buying a good business is tractable, but it's a slog. It takes endurance. It takes patience. It takes a willingness to look at deal after deal after deal and say "no" until you find the one that's right.

For me, the process wasn't a weekend project. It took two years. Even after identifying targets and getting serious, it still took over a year (actually closer to eighteen months for me) between LOI and closing on the first deal. That's not because the world is unfair. It's because this is a major transaction involving real people, real capital, and real due diligence.

You might review dozens of businesses and find nothing worth buying. That doesn't mean the entire market is a scam. It means you're hunting. And hunting is not shopping.

WHAT A BUSINESS-BUYING FUNNEL ACTUALLY LOOKS LIKE

The numbers set expectations. In my own funnel for my first business, it looked something like this:

- I reviewed roughly seventy-five businesses at the "signed NDA / saw financials" level (about fifteen of those were off-market).
- Of those seventy-five, I had broker calls on around forty.
- I spoke to around thirty sellers directly.
- I wrote LOIs for fifteen.
- I wrote one offer.
- I bought one business.

That ratio is clarifying, isn't it? If you believe you'll buy one of the first five listings you see, you are the person the market will punish. Which brings us to the final psychological trap that I want to end this chapter with.

THE URGENCY TRAP: Buying a Business Is *Not* Like Buying a House

Most people only make big purchases under urgency. You need a car because your old one died. You need a house because life changed. Your lease is ending. You're moving. And that urgency creates pressure. Pressure creates bad decisions. Bad decisions create "I got scammed" stories.

Business acquisition is different. You do not "need" to buy a business. Not in the same way, at least. And that's an advantage, if you use it correctly. When you start a business, you do have urgency:

you need customers quickly, you need revenue, you need to stop bleeding. But when you buy a business, if you bring that same urgency into acquisition, you will overpay or buy the wrong thing just to feel relief. You will buy business number four when the right business is number forty-four.

So one of the most important mindset shifts in this entire book is—

Give yourself time. Plan for a **multi**-year process. Decide that you are **hunting**, not shopping. This is an investment purchase, closer to buying a rental property than buying a primary residence.

Understand also that sellers will have emotions, too. Some will think their business is worth more because they built it. Some will resist protections because they want the payday. Some will be honest. Others, crooked. That's why due diligence is a thing. We can get you where it feels like you want to go now—owning a business—but we're going to take the best path we can. And now with our concerns handled and objections laid aside, we begin the journey with the first step to ownership—narrowing the buying scope.

CHAPTER 3

Narrowing Your Buying Scope: Price, Geography, and Industry

"GOOD, FAST, OR CHEAP—PICK ONE." This is pop-culture advice on product research. You're thinking about buying a given widget item, consumable, or service; you look up your options on Google Maps or Amazon or the like. What do the reviews say? What's the best value? Which are you least likely to regret? All this is under consideration. There is good quality, fast function (or delivery or effectiveness), or low price; most options offer basically one of these, a few purport to offer two of three, but none all three.

Buying a business reminds me of this. It's not that you're going to "pick two" but rather . . . *pick few*. As in, picky only a *few* constraints for which business(es) you'll consider buying. Because the more requirements you personally have going on, the higher the premium you're likely to pay. The good, fast, cheap rough equivalent for acquisition is price, industry, geography—the more flexible you are with each of these, the better deal on the best business you're likely to get. Conversely, the tighter you are on all three, the more you'll pay, and the longer you'll hunt.

Order of operations matters. The first constraint isn't a preference; it's math. Let's review.

START WITH PRICE: BECAUSE REALITY BEGINS WITH YOU

The one thing you can't talk your way out of is your current financial situation. You can't motivation-poster your way into a larger personal balance sheet or bigger down payment (if you can, let me know; you're going into business with me). Your money reality is what it is, so be honest about what you can bring to the negotiation table. I want you asking one blunt question: **How much money can I actually put into a deal right now?**

No wishing or hoping or praying, no best-case scenario imagination, and by that same token, no worst-case scenario amount you could scrape together everything by draining all accounts and fire-selling everything in your life in total panic. Keyword above is "actually." You ought to *want* to buy a business, and a want is not a need. You do not live in the cold exposed to the elements; a business is not a roof over your head. Be realistic. How much can you bring, liquid, without deluding yourself?

From there, you do the adult thing and talk to a bank. In an upcoming chapter, I'll talk about how to get a business loan prequalification so you'll know what you can borrow and under what terms. If you're thinking Small Business Administration financing, you'll want a lender who does these deals constantly—called an SBA preferred lender—because they know the rules and they'll tell you quickly what's realistic. Careful with SBA loans, however; you're personally guaranteeing anything you accept. If things go sideways, it's not like a car loan where the lender takes the car, end of story. With SBA debt, the collateral extends beyond the business to your house, your personal assets, and a court-ordered portion of your future earnings from when you have to crawl back to nine-to-five employment . . . everything is on the table. That's why there are limits on what the SBA will lend . . . and why there should be limits on what you are willing to buy.

So, price comes first because price defines your first boundary. Once you know the range you can realistically transact in, you'll never waste time daydreaming over deals you won't be able to close. If that range feels too small—if you look at your number and think, *I can't buy anything worth buying for that*—you don't cope by lying to yourself. You'll "cope" by acknowledging the real next lever—**outside capital**. Maybe that's family, a friend, a private individual (e.g., your step-dad who believes in you), or a professional investor (e.g., an "angel" investor). We'll talk about financing strategies later, in Chapter 5. The point here for now is that **price is the least flexible constraint, so accept it first.**

GEOGRAPHY: The Constraint We Pretend Is Flexible Until It Isn't

Once you know your price, you move to geography. Yes, there's personal preference here as well. Some places are "hard no." Most people wouldn't want to run a business in Juneau, Alaska, for example, even if you could hypothetically up and move there next month. You can be single, free, and unattached and still have places you will not live.

But in real life, geography isn't usually constrained by preference; it's constrained by **family**. Are you married? Kids in school? Does your spouse have a career tied to a location? Divorced and have custody arrangements? Does your family's best interest make cross-town much less cross-country movement impractical if not impossible? Factor it in.

And, yes, you need to show up in person for this new business you own. Don't sabotage yourself with unrealistic expectations. Aspirants will want the upside of business ownership without commitment to the physical presence that ownership requires. If you buy a business—especially using bank money or investor money—**you need to be where the business is**, at least at first. Investors will expect you to treat their money like your own. Banks expect you to be close enough to oversee what you bought. In many SBA situations, there are geographic limits in the underwriting; the lender knows you can't effectively supervise a business that's a five-hour flight away.

My rule of thumb is to be physically present three days a week minimum in the beginning, and to be prepared for the first year to demand more presence than I'd like. That may mean four days per week, e.g., Monday, Tuesday, Thursday, Friday. In some cases, five or six. In a few? Seven. Plus a few evenings. Maybe. Really? Yes. Go into this with your eyes wide open.

Eventually, you'll build systems and train leadership so you're not chained to the building, but the early phase is hands-on. Remember, the business is transitioning. People are watching you. The seller is fading out. The culture is trying to decide if you're real.

So, before you let yourself fall in love with a deal, ask yourself:

- *Will I commute like a normal job?*
- *Am I willing to do a long, big-city commute?*
- *Am I willing to fly there and stay three to four days per workweek?*

- *Am I willing to move?*

Then comes the most honest question of all:

- *Is there any scenario where I end up with millions on the line . . . and the only way to protect it is doing something I'm not willing to do?*

If the answer to that last question there is ever a "yes," you're probably setting yourself up for a disaster. Don't buy a deal that requires a life you don't want to live, now or after you close.

My own situation is the cleanest example of this constraint as real, not theoretical. I'm divorced, have joint custody of two kids, and see them half the time. That means I couldn't "just move" to wherever the best deal was. My kids need stability. Think school, support network, routine, all the basic stuff that matters more than my own entrepreneurial ambition.

So I drew a practical boundary—any businesses I buy needs to be within a reasonable morning and afternoon drive, or a very short regional airport flight away, roughly an hour to an hour and a half on way tops regardless of means of transport.

The wider your net, the better deal you can get and the more selective you can be in industry. The tighter your geographic net, the more you'll need to stay flexible somewhere else. Geography controls your options. Money may be mostly outside your control, so do what you can here to open them back up.

INDUSTRY: Where People Over-Constrain and Accidentally Tax Themselves

Industry options are where most "wantrepreneurs" make the mistake of **emotion**. They decide what they "really want," narrow too early, then pay a premium for the privilege of being picky. You can do that. But understand what you're doing. Over-constraining industry is like opening up a home-buying search website and setting the results to an exact neighborhood, one specific housing development, a certain price . . . and it has to have a white picket fence. Good luck. Your options collapse. You won't see enough inventory. You won't develop judgment. You'll either freeze for months (years?) or overpay—then or now. Just put up the fence yourself, OK?

I've already told you I recommend gray-collar and blue-collar-type businesses. My two (and two only) industry selection rules will give my best reasons why you should follow this recommendation, too.

THE FIRST INDUSTRY SELECTION RULE: Avoid Easy-Startup Businesses

If a business can be started with $50,000 (or less), two men, and one truck, then you should seriously ask why you'd buy it at a premium in the first place and not just start your own damn business. Roofing is the classic example. It's not that roofing can't make money; the barrier to entry is low. Very low. Too low. You can get one contract, take a deposit, order materials when, and congratulations . . . you own a roofing company. Risk is relatively low and the starting capital is relatively small.

Easy-to-start businesses result in the entire industry getting overrun by competition, pushing prices down, and squeezing profit margins. There is no moat guarding your business-castle. If it's easy for you, it's easy for the next guy, too.

As with roofing, the restaurant business has a low barrier to entry. Margins are thin, they're hard to run, and the failure rate is famously brutal. Even sophisticated buyers get tired of restaurants;

unit economics are unforgiving. The business can be so hands-on and finicky that stepping away for a month can turn into a fire.

Since you're looking to buy a business for long-term ownership, then the businesses you should be wary of share two traits—low barrier to entry and thin margins that punish mistakes. My first rule here rules them out.

THE SECOND INDUSTRY SELECTION RULE: Avoid "Hot" Industries With Deep-Pocket Buyers

This is the opposite of easy. Some industries are so in-demand that your competition isn't other individuals looking to buy, it's **private equity**. Now, *public* equity is when a business sells shares on a public exchange, i.e., the stock market, but *private* equity is when a business sells shares privately, usually to a firm that raised money from wealthy individuals, institutions, pension funds, or family offices. The basic acquisition-by-private-equity play looks like this:

- Private equity (PE) raises a fund.
- PE buys multiple businesses over several years.
- PE restructures the separate businesses into a single venture.
- PE streamlines operations, consolidates overhead, and lays off up to 75 percent of all staff across the previously-separate businesses bought from individual owner-sellers.
- PE rolls up the business and resells to enjoy return on investment (ROI), around five to seven years after the first acquisition in the space.

Private equity is big money. Money talks. Private equity is loud.

In my region—the Southeast—HVAC and plumbing became the poster children for PE roll-ups. Private equity realized something that sounds obvious in hindsight—in Atlanta in July, when it's 95 degrees with 95 percent humidity, if your AC breaks, you don't wait out the market. You find the money. Such demand is recession-resistant. It's urgent and non-optional. HVAC also has a built-in recurring service layer—install the unit today, and you're the company the homeowner calls when it fails later. Even if new home construction slows, the repair and maintenance demand can still pay the bills and put profit on the books.

Private equity also knows how to industrialize lead flow via search engine optimization (SEO), paid search, call centers, dispatch, conversion, and so on. All marketing and sales becomes a math problem, i.e., how much does a lead cost and what's the close rate?

Then come the synergies I talked about; PE will buy, for example, one HVAC company in Charlotte and another in Greensboro and suddenly the back office can consolidate scheduling, call center, and administration. Roll-ups create efficiency across both marketing and management, and that efficiency becomes pure profit. This is why "hot" industries trade at higher multiples. You're not just paying for cashflow; you're paying for the fact that everyone else wants that very same cashflow, too.

If you want only HVAC and plumbing, you can do that, yeah, but you're voluntarily walking into a premium market where you're competing against people who have $250 million in a fund and a five-to-seven-year flip plan.

If you want the best deal, don't over-constrain industry. Pickiness becomes a tax you pay.

The one potential saving grace is the **psychology of selling to private equity**. Let's talk about that.

Most of these owners selling businesses at present and in the near future amid the great baby boomer retirement are emotionally attached to the company. It's their baby. It's their legacy. Many do not love the idea of selling to some banker in New York who doesn't know the business, doesn't care about the employees, and is simply flipping a spreadsheet inside a larger machine. They probably have no intention to visit the company in person beyond the first day of ownership! They'll drop in the week after closing, shake hands with everyone, disappear by lunch time, and before anyone remembers the new owner's name . . . his PE firm has laid off half the staff, including favorite-employee Cindy who's worked here since she was nineteen years old (she's fifty-six now). Private equity doesn't care.

This is where you, as an individual buyer, have a legitimate advantage as a buyer opposite private equity. You can position yourself as a steward not a strip-miner. You're the person who wants to keep the name, honor the legacy, keep the employees (especially Cindy), and run the thing for the long term.

I beat multiple private equity bidders for his first acquisition specifically because the seller didn't want to hand the company over to an out-of-town flip plan. So, again private equity can outspend you and probably will if this is your first rodeo. But they can't out-*meaning* you—if you know how to sell yourself as the right successor. Sometimes, a fair price from the right person beats the highest price from the wrong buyer.

WHERE GEOGRAPHY AND INDUSTRY MEET: Follow Growth

Now we blend the second and third constraints, geography and industry. One of the best ways to find durable demand is to look at what's expanding:

- Where are people moving?

- Where are new housing developments going up?
- Where are home builds increasing?
- Where are rent prices rising (a signal of housing pressure)?

If rents spike, you're probably not losing inventory. People are coming in. That means you'll need everything that supports population growth: utilities, schools, hospitals, maintenance services, trades, and infrastructure.

This is also where industry choices can become logical instead of emotional. I once looked at a well-digging company in Spartanburg, South Carolina, because the geographic trend made it make sense. That corridor was growing, people were moving in, and city utilities weren't expanding fast enough into rural areas. If water infrastructure won't reach the sticks soon, wells remain necessary. That created a credible growth path for that business in that region.

Would the same business make sense somewhere else? Maybe not. A well-digging company in Trenton, New Jersey, felt like a dying premise—different infrastructure, different density, different need. So you're not really asking, *What business do I want to buy and run?* You're asking, *In this geography, over the next decade, what services will people obviously need?*

Beyond residential growth, there's another signal to find amid the noise especially for commercial and infrastructure-heavy work—**cheap energy and business-friendly conditions**.

Manufacturing and data centers are energy-intensive. Large companies place big bets where power is abundant and affordable and where tax and regulatory incentives are favorable. Those projects are often publicly visible. Think announced developments, public works, big capital expenditures you can literally read about.

So again, the two broad signal categories where geography

and industry overlap to give you a favorable start to your search are;

- Population growth (residential demand plus commercial services that follow people)
- Cheap power and favorable policy (manufacturing, data centers, industrial growth)

All that said, growth can raise prices, too. A high-growth region can attract so many buyers that you pay more for the same cashflow. In some cases, you might find a better deal in a slower-growth place simply because fewer buyers want to live there. That doesn't automatically make it a bad investment, it just changes the kind of upside you're pursuing.

A QUICK DETOUR: Micro "Businesses" That Are Really Just Products

At some point, every buyer sees these distractions: $13,000 for a "cashflowing website," $6,800 for an "e-commerce store," $1,200 for a functional app that is just now post-revenue. The listings are clean and the pitch is a dream. Some call these microacquisitions or microbusinesses.

Who cares. We've got a problem. Many of these are not businesses in the way I mean it in this book. They're often products built by someone with technical skill, front-loading their profit by selling the "asset" before the market shifts, the traffic dies, or the competition squeezes it into nothing. So the question to ask is the same one you should ask anywhere:

> If it really was hands-off and durable, why are they selling it?

Often the answer is because they can collect a year's worth of profit today, in one check, by offloading the decay risk to you. The deeper issue is the same as roofing. If the marginal cost and barrier to entry are low, the market gets crowded. Crowded markets race to the bottom. Moat-less businesses don't stay moat-less forever—they get copied, undercut, and replaced. If you're buying for something lasting, you need a moat, some kind of barrier that prevents any ole Joe Schmo from undercutting you tomorrow.

FROM INFINITE OPTIONS TO NARROW OPPORTUNITY

The point of all this price, geography, and industry business isn't to box you in; it's to stop you from wasting time. If you open a broker site—BizBuySell, DealStream, whatever—you'll see everything, like gas stations, manufacturing, car washes, event venues, niche services, trades, boutiques, and plenty of businesses that are basically just jobs for sale. If you try to evaluate "everything," you'll evaluate nothing. So when the time comes, use high-level filters:

- Price range that's real for you
- Geography you can actually operate within
- Industries you won't touch, and industries you're open to

Reduce your list to something small enough that you can actually give it attention. If I handed you ten thousand stacks of paper and told you to evaluate them one by one, you'd never get to the NDA stage, never get to an offer, never get to closing. Never.

Once you've narrowed your scope the right way—without lying to yourself and without over-constraining your options—you're ready for the next phase, which is learning the rules and red flags that keep you from wasting months on the wrong deal when you thought you had it all figured out.

To put that another way, price, geography, and industry matter more than just about any other factor. *Just about*. As with any high-dollar sale, the devil lies in the details. Let's see them now.

CHAPTER 4

Rules and Red Flags While Business Shopping

LET ME TELL YOU ABOUT THE BUSINESS I ALMOST bought. It was an electrical business in South Carolina. On paper, it looked strong. Revenue was good. Net income looked good also. The story was growth, that this thing is working and would continue to so you'd better get in quick before the asking price goes higher.

But right away, it was that very asking price that gave me pause. The owners were asking for five times their *best* year, which just so happened to be their most recent year. That's a premium. And premiums aren't automatically wrong. Premiums just have to be justified. This one, I ultimately didn't think was.

Most sellers looking to pull a fast one on you don't bring you their average year. As a general rule, I'm not pricing a deal off of one year. I'm looking at a **three-year average**, and I'm comparing the multiple to what's typical for that industry. A lot of blue- and gray-collar trades sit in a broad range like three to five times EBITDA of the average of the last three years, but the exact number changes with heat, geography, and buyer competition. Needless to say, pricing based on the best year, the most recent year, made me suspicious. Gross profit margin all but confirmed it.

Let me give you some foundational knowledge about gross profits with this hypothetical. Suppose I add a million dollars of top line revenue. That could be through better marketing, streamlined operations, higher-motivated salespeople… or it could be they took jobs at cost. If the latter, what does any of that do for me? I need to see the gross profit margin on that revenue, for one thing. Did they just goose revenue but not make more money? Now, in the current business I've bought and run—commercial electrical—a 28.4 percent gross margin is a great number. That's what mine is. It's a most-companies-would-kill-for-that number. But that South Carolina business was presenting something just above a 40 percent gross profit margin. Can you hear the alarm bells?

I did. That said, *sometimes* gross margin *appears* inflated for a reason that's fixable down later in the accounting. Sometimes, an owner miscategorizes expenses. Sometimes, they shove costs that should be Cost Of Goods Sold, called COGS, elsewhere. Perhaps a project manager who really exists to run jobs might be sitting in an overhead expenses category when they should be allocated to COGS because that makes more sense. If that's what's happening, it doesn't mean the business is a scam; it means the financial presentation needs adjustments. So while I was on high alert as I read this company's financials, I also let myself breathe a little and take my time because it could be a false alarm. What I did believe with as much certainty as I could, however, was that this business did *not* have a 40-plus percent gross profit margin, so a five-times multiple was *not* going to work for me.

Then I started asking about transition plans. The owners didn't have one. Oh, really? You want to retire and be done with it as soon as possible? A business this profitable? Your best year ever, and you want out? So then I asked for what I always want when I'm serious—monthly balance sheets for at least the last twenty-four months.

And there it is . . .

They'd moved receivables (revenue coming in) and payables (expenses going out) between years—shifting the dates of both around to make the gross profit margin look better than it really was. So there was no clean reconciliation between what they were telling a prospective buyer (me) and what the business would have had to show in reality were the owners fully honest. Integrity-free business dealings have a bigger problem than the buyer (me again) who walks away (I did)—the IRS. It's one thing to get "creative" to inflate your company's value; it's another to engage in something like fraud in your tax returns.

The week after I wrote this chapter, an anonymous HVAC business listing on a brokerage website went viral because the cash flow was on average just under $1 million. But what's called the **Seller's Discretionary Earnings** (SDE) percentage was about 50 percent. SDE is the total cash benefit an owner-operator gets from the business in a year. It's the owner's true take-home number that, if you know anything about taxes, is basically the owner's *pre-tax, almost-net profit*. An accountant may get fickle over my wording, but that's directionally accurate for our purposes here, which is to note . . . *no* HVAC business has a 50 percent SDE margin. None. Net profit in a *good* HVAC business is anywhere between 10 and 25 percent, likely no higher. The listing screamed scam, and one of my favorite exchanges in the replies on the post calling it out went like this:

Looks turnkey.

You'll be turning a key for sure.

Maybe to the storage locker you have to buy to live in after losing your house.

At this stage of your business search, that is exactly your

frame—*I am looking for businesses that will crash, burn, and leave me king of the ash heap.*

Wait . . . looking for such bad-deal businesses? Is that a misprint? No. I'll explain.

THE KEY TO YOUR SEARCH: Look for Businesses You're Not Looking For

Most first-time buyers think their business search is about finding great businesses. It's not.

Think of it like Google. You type in your keywords—in the case of shopping for businesses, that'd be price, geography, industry. Then, you see search results. What do you do with search results? You're not trying to click everything. You're scanning to eliminate what you're not going to click.

Get it? I'm sure you do. Your business search is not to find good businesses to potentially buy. Your business search is to find businesses to rule out—fast—so you can invest your time, attention, and resources only into the few that are worth deeper diligence. That's what rules and red flags are—a funnel. Automatic outs. A disciplined way to avoid wasting months chasing a mirage. Wise.

So, below are the **Red Flags** you should be looking for while you shop—and each one closes with a **Rule** for what to do about it every single time.

THE 13 RED FLAGS (AND THE RULE FOR EACH)

Pay attention so you don't get scammed, screwed, or—worst of all—audited by the IRS.

RED FLAG: An Unjustified Premium Price

A premium isn't automatically wrong. But if a seller is pricing at the top end—or beyond it—based on a best-year-ever story, you need to know exactly what you're paying for. In most trades, you don't price off one great year. You look at a three-year average and then apply the appropriate multiple for that industry.

RULE

If the asking price is above the normal multiple for that industry, demand a clear justification—and price off a multi-year average, not the best year. If the justification is "trust me," walk.

RED FLAG: GROSS PROFIT MARGIN THAT DOESN'T PASS A DOUBLE-CHECK

Gross margin is one of your fastest lie detectors. If a seller's gross margin is materially different from the industry norm, something is going on: miscategorized costs, a temporary sweetheart contract, underreported labor, deferred expenses, or outright manipulation.

RULE:

Know typical gross margins for the industry you're shopping and treat "materially higher than normal" as a forced-explanation event. If you can't reconcile it quickly with credible detail, move on.

RED FLAG: EXPENSE CATEGORY GAMES AND FINANCIALS THAT DON'T RECONCILE

If you have to squint to understand how the business actually makes money, that's not complexity. That's . . . risky. When you request monthly balance sheets and you can't reconcile them—especially across year boundaries—assume someone is telling you a curated version of the truth.

RULE:

Require monthly financials and tax returns, and insist they reconcile in a coherent way. If the books can't be explained cleanly—or the seller stalls—treat it as an automatic out.

RED FLAG: CUSTOMER CONCENTRATION (I.E., ONE CLIENT IS 30-PLUS PERCENT OF NET REVENUE)

Any business living off a few customers is fragile. Lose one relationship and you can lose a third of your business overnight. Sometimes this is OK, like with a landscaping company with an enforceable contract that transfers with the sale. But often it's not a contract. In many of the businesses you'll be looking at, contracts are handshakes. The paper trail is memories of conversations. So, no trail at all. The contract is just a relationship with the owner and the client's late father (rest in peace). So, when the owner leaves, the sentimentality ends, and the business is all gone.

RULE:

If one customer is more than 30 percent of revenue, either **(a)** you have enforceable contractual protection, or **(b)** you restructure the deal to protect yourself (earn-out, seller financing, longer transition). If the seller wants to vanish immediately and you're exposed, walk away.

RED FLAG: DECLINING YEAR-OVER-YEAR REVENUE (OR PROFITABILITY)

Stagnant isn't necessarily bad—especially with a boomer owner who hasn't pushed growth in years. Steady can be beautiful. Decline is different. Decline means you need a real explanation: is it the owner taking their foot off the gas, or are customers dying off, markets shifting, and the business losing relevance?

RULE:

Treat sustained decline as a problem until proven otherwise. If you can't explain the decline—and how you'll reverse it without fantasy—walk. If it's steady and simply under-optimized, that can be a buy signal.

RED FLAG: SKETCHY TAX STRATEGY (OR HIDDEN DEBT)

Some owners do weird things to avoid taxes. Sometimes they "loan themselves" large sums from the business. That doesn't just evaporate. Someone owes taxes on that. And if you buy the business without cleaning it up, you can inherit the blast radius.

RULE:

Assume nothing is harmless until your accountant verifies it. If you see odd loans, odd liabilities, overdue supplier payments, or anything that smells like accounting gymnastics, bring in an accountant and make resolution a condition of closing.

RED FLAG: A VAGUE (OR SUSPICIOUS) REASON FOR SELLING

"I'm seventy-four, I'm tired, I don't have kids to pass this to."

That makes sense. But a fifty-three-year-old claiming "I just want to retire" with no actual justification—and wanting an abbreviated transition—should make you cautious. Especially if key employees are their relatives. When the purpose doesn't make sense, everything else becomes less believable. As it should.

RULE:

If the seller's motivation doesn't add up, assume there's more you're not being told. In that scenario, adopt the operating posture: believe nothing else they say. It's not "trust but verify." It's "distrust so verify."

RED FLAG: IT WAS LISTED BEFORE (OR WAS UNDER LOI) AND FELL THROUGH

If a prior buyer got far enough to sign an LOI and then walked, they discovered something they didn't like. Maybe the buyer was unreasonable and tried to retrade the deal. That happens. But you need a straight answer.

RULE:

Ask directly, "Has this been under LOI before? Why did it fall through?" If the explanation is vague, evasive, or inconsistent, assume the prior buyer found something material—and you'll either find it after spending time and money, or you won't find it until it's too late.

RED FLAG: HIGH EMPLOYEE TURNOVER

Turnover is culture leaking out. You want to know how many employees, what roles, and average tenure—especially for key people. If your average tenure is eighteen months or less, you're dealing with churn. And churn means you'll be constantly replacing people, constantly rehiring, constantly retraining.

Amazon famously structured stock vesting cliffs around the reality that average tenure was short. If your workforce behaves like that—people don't stick—there's usually a reason. By the way, the very week I wrote this chapter, Amazon announced an additional 16,000 layoffs—this following 14,000 layoffs announced just three months prior at the time of this writing. The reason given was to "strengthen our organization by reducing layers, increasing ownership, and removing bureaucracy."[6] But the likeliest suspect, most in-the-know insiders believe, is AI. AI is taking jobs and killing careers. Upwards of 30,000 more people now need this book right away.

RULE:

Treat low average tenure as a warning light. If key roles can't be retained, either the business is underpaying, overworking, mismanaged, or unstable. Price the risk accordingly—or walk.

---

6 Annie Palmer, "Amazon Laying Off About 16,000 Corporate Workers in Latest Anti-Bureaucracy Push," CNBC, January 28, 2026, https://www.cnbc.com/2026/01/28/amazon-layoffs-anti-bureaucracy-ai.html.

RED FLAG: LAWSUITS, LEGAL TROUBLE, AND PATTERNS OF CONFLICT

If there's one lawsuit in ten years and it's clearly explained and resolved, that can be the exception. If there are multiple, you're not buying a business . . . you're buying someone else's litigation lifestyle. In the worst case, you're buying a law firm partner's next supercar.

RULE:

One resolved, well-explained issue may be acceptable with attorney review and deal protections. A pattern is an automatic "no." And if it's unresolved with large potential liability, don't kid yourself—talk to counsel and be willing to walk.

RED FLAG: REPUTATION ISSUES (BAD REVIEWS, BAD PRESS, CONSUMER COMPLAINTS)

A two-star average with dozens of reviews is not something you just ignore. But you also don't panic blindly. Sometimes the seller is a boomer who never managed their online presence. Sometimes competitors post garbage. Sometimes only angry customers leave reviews. The real question is: what does the underlying customer reality look like?

If the owner has been actively managing marketing and reputation and it's still bad, that's a problem. If the business has healthy recurring customers and the owner hasn't been managing online presence, it may be fixable. Unusually high customer churn plus external hate usually means the hate is earned.

I want you to understand something: **If the current owner isn't actively managing the business, the business will actively manage you when you buy it.**

RULE:

Decide whether you're looking at **(a)** an outward-facing marketing problem you can fix, or **(b)** an inward-facing service or culture problem that will eat you alive. If the business is bleeding customers and the reputation is ugly, walk. If recurring customers are strong and the online presence is neglected, price in cleanup and move forward carefully.

RED FLAG: A BUSINESS BEING RESOLD

If this is your first business, don't buy a business that was recently bought and is already back on the market. That is the red flag *and* the rule. Because either the original seller hid something, or the buyer ran it poorly, or the business is harder than it looks, or customers and employees got burned during the transition. In real estate, sometimes you can point to a cracked foundation and price it. In business, the problems are often subjective and intractable—reputation, culture, customer trust, employee stability. It's more like drilling for oil in a field you don't understand than it is repairing a known defect.

RULE:

As a first-time buyer, treat "recently bought, now selling" as a hard no. No exceptions. None.

CAVEAT:

If this is not your first business, and if you're experienced and you're in the same industry with real downside protection—employees and assets you can absorb, overlap you can leverage—then and only then ought you investigate. Otherwise, you're signing up for maximum downside with minimal clarity. Just say no!

RED FLAG: DELUSION, NOT CONVICTION

This is a mismatch between passion and opportunity. I'll explain.

If you're going into your first acquisition with one foot out—like a "best I could do" marriage—don't do it. You need conviction, because you're going to hit stress, friction, unexpected problems, and moments where quitting is tempting. But conviction doesn't mean sexy. In fact, the sexiest businesses are often the worst buys, because people fall in love with the story and stop being objective.

The late great author, humorist, and serial entrepreneur Scott Adams has an anecdote from his banking days that I think about a lot—the most passionate founders seeking funding were often the highest risk. The boring operators with boring businesses were often the safest bets. And there's truth in that, because passion can cloud judgment the same way falling in love with a dream home can make you overpay and ignore the facts.

The correct order of operations not to get scammed goes like so:

1. Watch out for red flags.
2. Obey the rules when you see one.
3. Cultivate your energy for the right opportunity that passes all the filters.

Now, this is what I mean by proper conviction: *Do I believe in this business like an entrepreneurial Santa Claus, or am I really excited about solving its real, confirmed problems and maximizing its missed opportunities?*

Very different questions, very different outcomes. That's why some of my favorite businesses are painfully unsexy. A jetting and drain-cleaning company with municipal contracts? Boring. But it can be wildly profitable. A company that replaces telephone poles? Also very boring. Until a hurricane drops 5,000 poles and the business absolutely PRINTS because it has the contracts, trucks, and inventory.

Do not chase cool; chase what works. But first, you'll have to chase out of town any options that are definitely a not-it.

NEXT UP . . . SELLING YOURSELF AS A BUYER

Once you're filtering with discipline—and ruling out landmines—you run into your next problem—**even if you find a great business, why should anyone sell it to you?** That's where we go next . . . how to sell yourself as a buyer. First to the bank, then to the seller.

We'll go there next, but first, let's give you what I promised—examples of businesses bought and not bought, and why.

CHAPTER 5

Deal, or No Deal?

THERE IS SOMETHING MADDENING ABOUT BUYING a business, be it your first, or your tenth. I'm not yet at ten businesses bought or sold, but because I'm following my own advice laid out in this very book, I don't expect it will be long before that is the case for me. At any rate, given the entrepreneurs I talk to across the US, this observation does hold regardless of your own experience. Your mileage probably will not vary. It goes like this:

> A good business can look terrible on paper; a bad business can look amazing on paper.

The most deceptive word in acquisitions is "obviously." For example, "obviously" that's a bad deal. Or "obviously," this seller is telling the truth. "Obviously," the tax returns are close enough, and "obviously" the broker disclosed what I need to know, therefore "obviously" the numbers will work once I'm the owner. There's an account on the 𝕏 platform called @JoshuaLisec that is pretty widely known for mocking what he calls "badverbs." That's where someone with a hidden agenda uses adverbs to deceive others, whether in politics or news media or in business. If you start hearing a broker or a seller using "-ly" adverbs, then what you see on paper may not be what you get. The inverse may also be true. Suppose legal counsel whom you hire tells you the deal you're considering is "truly" terrible "actually." There may be a lot more to it than meets the eye. Chapter 4's rules and red flags are the best starting and continuing point. But sometimes, even oftentimes, you'll find reality offers up an advanced lesson that just might reveal loopholes in those rules and camouflage on those flags. And to illustrate, let me tell you about a business I bought—and one I didn't—and why.

At the end of the day, what we're pursuing is not a business we like—it's a business we can prove that is what it says it is, and if not, what it really is instead.

THE BUSINESS I BOUGHT

The first company I ended up buying did not look like a dream business when I first saw it. It's the commercial electrical contractor I've told you a bit about already. Now, its premise was promising—commercial electrical work is real-world, physical, difficult to automate, locally embedded, operationally complex, and necessary. Buildings need power, projects need wiring, equipment needs installation, facilities need maintenance, and at least for the medium term, ChatGPT is going to do precisely none of that.

That said, the category made sense, but the numbers looked sketchy. At first glance, the historical income statement showed negative EBITDA (that's Earnings Before Interest, Taxes, Depreciation, and Amortization) in two prior years, then a major improvement later—at the very time the owner happened to be selling. Obviously, that's a trick. No deal, obviously.

Obviously?

See, if you look only at the surface-level income statement, you'd walk away. I wondered if what we might have here is an owner who tried to minimize his tax liabilities year after year, then suddenly decided he wanted to sell the business and remade his tax strategy to boost everything on paper. What if both numbers, those of the bad years and those of that one good one, were both wrong and the truth lay somewhere in the middle?

I did my due digging. One of the first things I looked at was gross profit margin. The business was showing gross margins that bounced all over the place; one year it was around 21.5 percent. Another year it was around 23 percent. Then around 18 percent. Then the seller was projecting something more like 25 percent going forward. Well, which is it? What's the real gross profit margin of this company? Changing the gross profit margin assumption by a few percentage points can create or destroy hundreds of thousands of dollars in modeled EBITDA. In the model I built, moving from the seller's more optimistic projection based on that one fudgy year to what I believed was a more accurate margin could create roughly a half-million-dollar difference.

Now multiply that across multiple years. Then multiply the difference by the valuation multiple. Then finance it with debt. Then personally guarantee it. Welcome to business buying.

WHEN CRAP NUMBERS HIDE A GOLD BUSINESS

My hunch proved correct. The owner had indeed been running his commercial contracting company like an Internet bro's lifestyle hustle. The company wasn't fake, mind you, it just means the financial statements were not cleanly designed to help a buyer understand the true earning power of the company. Turns out, a lot of owner-operators run businesses this way for decades. They care about making money, paying fewer taxes, and taking care of their families. They do not care about preparing clean, buyer-friendly financial statements three years before a sale . . . until they absolutely do and care about nothing else besides getting the highest-possible asking price in hopes no buyer notices what really went on before the owner decided to sell and make the spreadsheets look pretty and profitable.

In the contractor's case, the stated owner add-backs were not enough to explain what was happening inside the company. The numbers still did not quite make sense. So I looked at sample jobs—I looked for cleaner examples, jobs that were not contaminated by the owner's personal expenses or miscategorized costs. I wanted to understand what a real, normalized job looked like. After doing that, I came to believe the company's true gross profit margin was not 18 percent. It was not even the seller's projected 25 percent. I believed a reasonable number was closer to 28 percent.

Whoa . . .

Either I was wrong, in which case this business was worth very little and could lose me a lot of money. Or . . . I was right, in which case this business was worth a lot more than it appeared to be worth.

There was not much middle ground. And that was scary.

In my model, I believed the business could produce around $2 million in EBITDA. I also modeled growth. If we could get the company to around $15 million in revenue, I believed adjusted EBITDA could land around $2.6 million.

And after I bought it, in the first year, the business did over $15 million in revenue and adjusted EBITDA came in around $2.68 million.

I wasn't correct; I was *over*-correct.

It was worth it. I'd end up buying the company for $4.9 million. Of that, $2.7 million was financed through an SBA loan, and $1.6 million was seller financing. If you had looked only at the company's unadjusted income statement, there was no way to justify paying that purchase price. No sane person would pay nearly $5 million for a business if the basic income statement were the whole story.

But I wasn't buying the surface financials . . . was I?

This is important: When you make an initial offer or submit an indication of interest, you are not marrying the deal; you are buying time. Then diligence begins. Then you can determine if what you'll see is what you'll get and it may be "obviously" a bad deal at that point, or "absolutely" not. Let the real numbers guide you, keep digging, and trust your experts—whom you're paying well. I did, and it all paid off.

What if I hadn't?

THE BUSINESS I DIDN'T

Another business I looked at was another commercial electrical contractor. On paper, this one looked absolutely excellent (that was my hint).

Could an unusually skilled operator achieve unusually high margins for this industry? Sure, and that's the story these numbers seemed to be telling me. It can happen. But when numbers are materially better than industry expectations, the burden of proof shifts. The seller has some explaining to do.

So I went and I asked the questions—all the questions. Of the seller, the broker, everyone.

> *Why are your margins this high? Are your labor costs categorized correctly? Are job costs sitting where they belong? Are project managers in overhead when they should be in cost of goods sold? Are you pushing costs into a later period? Are you pulling revenue forward? Are the financial*

statements consistent with the tax returns? Are you telling me the same story you told the IRS?

My basis for all questions of concern were as follows: The company appeared to be moving costs and revenue between years. Revenue was being counted in ways that made one period look better. Expenses were being shifted in ways that made another period look cleaner. The result was a business that looked more profitable every year than it really was—or was it? Was it not? Nope . . . turns out it was.

Eventually, the broker effectively admitted what was going on, maybe because I was a questioning pest more than anything. Indeed, the owner had been shifting expenses between years, counting things one way for seller presentation and another way elsewhere. The result was that the story being told to buyers did not reconcile with the story being told to the IRS.

New rule: If the financial statements and tax returns cannot be reconciled, stop. And so I did.

Good businesses, a *true* good business (notice I didn't "truly"), can survive scrutiny. One held up to seem so likely will not. You must resist the charm of the dream—how amazing entrepreneurship via acquisition is and can be. After patient analysis and only patient analysis will the truth emerge.

You may be surprised by what you eventually buy. And if you follow this book, then that's a good thing.

CHAPTER 6

Cash, Loans, Both, or Neither?

BUYING A BUSINESS CAN LEAD TO A LOT OF SPINE-tingle moments where you all of a sudden freeze up. You've thought about doing this, thought long and hard, but before you realize it, the moment has come. Second-guessing is a term that puts it lightly. More like . . . a potential crash-out.

> *Wait, what the f— am I doing?! What do I really know about this business anyway? How am I actually going to pay for this thing?*

It's usually the money issue that does it. The real estate mindset doesn't really help. That's what most future business buyers bring to the negotiation table because that's all most of us have known previously. The residential investor, even just the one-time home buyer, thus thinks of a business they might acquire along the lines of, *If I can pay cash, I should . . . I should put as much down as possible . . . then I should pay the loan off as fast as possible.*

That's how a lot of people think about mortgages, whether owning or renting out. But a business is not a house. A business has payroll, customers, and cashflow that can fluctuate month to month.

If you cut it too close to the bone, one bad quarter can put you in an even worse spot. All this gets forgotten in panic mode when your brain defaults to what you've always known that ain't so—a business is a house but it's not.

So here's how I want you to think about it now, so you can rethink it later when the pressure starts to cook because you're shopping for real. Your new perspective goes like this: *A loan isn't debt; it's flexibility.*

I'll explain what I mean. If you can put more down, the question is, should you? There is a world where you put too much cash into the deal, and now you have no margin for error. And then you're not just thinking, *Can I make my loan payment?* You're now ruminating hard in depressive mania. *Can I make payroll? I can. Can I pay vendors? No. Wait. Yes! No . . . And can I keep the lights on? Absolutely! . . . not. Oh, s—.* That's not where I want you to be.

If everything's going really well and you build up enough cash where you can pay the loan off and still have excess liquidity, then OK, great. Not a problem. Also not your expectation. Or shouldn't be. I don't want you to be so bare-bones because you put in all your rainy-day savings and literally every last dime of personal capital that one bad quarter means, *Now I can't make my SBA loan payment... and now I can't make payroll... and now I can't do those kinds of things.*

So, make sure you have margin for error in your personal financial situation—and in the business—so when it hits the fan, you have a money umbrella to keep from getting sprayed till it stops. And if you do, then it will.

Reality-check firmly aside now, let's get to the specifics—how to actually fund your business purchase.

THREE WAYS TO GET CAPITAL: Cash, Loans, Investors

At a high level, you basically have three ways to fund a deal:

- All cash (or mostly cash)
- Loans (Small Business Administration or conventional commercial)
- Outside investors (equity partners)

Many real-world deals are some blend of all three. I want you to understand what each option actually costs you—financially and psychologically—and what it demands from you. I've covered the too-mush-cash risk already from the outset, so let's talk about the next-most common money used for a small business—**SBA loans**.

These are the most realistic paths to buying a solid small business without already being wealthy. Even though SBA interest rates can be a little higher, SBA loans are usually amortized over ten years, and that longer runway matters because it lowers your monthly payment and gives you more flexibility. Compare that to a traditional commercial loan that might be five years.

Even if the interest rate is lower, your monthly payment can be dramatically higher because you're compressing the payoff period. There's a big difference between a $20,000 monthly payment and a $40,000 monthly payment. When you own a small business—where income can fluctuate—you want financial room to breathe.

The Down Payment Rule: Equity Injection

If you're getting a commercial loan—SBA or not—the lender is probably going to want an equity injection. For the SBA, 10 percent is generally the minimum, and some lenders want 15 or 20 percent. It's the same logic as a down payment on a house—it protects the lender and proves you're invested. Finally, real estate and business buying have something in common.

OK, so, anyway . . . let's say you're buying a business for $5 million. Then you'll need to be able to come up with at least $500,000. That can be your money or it can be an investor's money. But it's got to be somebody's. And probably not the seller's. This thing called **seller financing** no longer "counts" like it used to.

Now, this is important. There was a time when you could structure seller financing into the deal, and the SBA would count that seller note as part of the equity injection. For example—say you buy a $5 million business, get the seller to finance $1 million, and now it looks like a 20 percent equity injection.

That's how it looked until late 2025 when rules changed. Now, seller financing only counts as equity injection if the seller note is fully deferred for the entire life of the SBA loan, which is typically ten years. That means the seller gets paid no principal and no interest until a decade later. Good luck finding a seller who's willing to say, "Yeah, sure, pay me in ten years."

Yes, you can still do what are called **seller notes**—and I highly advise seller notes but not because they count for equity injection anymore. Seller notes:

- Lower how much you need to borrow from the bank,
- Often get better terms from the seller than the bank, and
- Can keep the seller incentivized during transition.

Even so, you should plan on being able to **bring at least 10 percent in real equity**.

Outside Investors: Less Than 20 Percent For Each Investor (Besides You)

If you bring in an investor, they'll want equity. Assuming you have an SBA loan, you have to follow their guidelines on percentage ownership.

According to the SBA, If an investor owns 20 percent or more of the company, they have to sign the personal guarantee—meaning they can come after any and all owners' personal finances, accounts, and access if the business fails. But if someone owns, say 19.5 percent, they do not have to be on the personal guarantee.

Now, you could have multiple investors—two at 10 percent is fine—because the SBA cares about each individual being under 20 percent. And by the way, the SBA has citizenship rules here; investors need to be U.S. citizens to be equity owners.

OK, let's say you're going to be able to bring 10 percent of the business asking price. If you have $50,000 personally to play with, that means you can buy a $500,000 business. It's going to be more like a micro business than a small business, but you get the point from the math. Now you've got two spots for longtime friends or mentors who believe in you, and now for 10 percent and 10 percent you're at 30 percent of the acquisition budget.

I mentioned seller notes. Can you get a loan from the seller of the business? Perhaps, but not in a payment-deferment sort of way. I mean an actual, real, commercial loan. It's as if they're participating in the financing just like your colleagues I mentioned in the last paragraph. Can they bring 10 percent? Possibly, as that enables them to help transition their "baby," so to speak.

What's relevant for you to know is that seller loan terms are likely going to be better than what you get from the SBA. You will probably need to get the rest from the SBA, to be clear, but let's cover as much of the price *before* going to the federal government so you're decreasing your own personal risk (don't forget about that personal guarantee . . .).

Now, there's a minimum interest rate concept called **AFR**—the **Applicable Federal Rate**—which is the minimum interest rate the IRS considers a legitimate loan. If you try to do below AFR, you can create tax problems because the IRS doesn't treat it like a real loan. So, do AFR (whatever it is at the time of your acquisition, say 4.5 or 4.75 percent realistically), and in a higher inflation environment, that rate can be attractive.

Adding it all up in this example, let's say we're now at 40 percent of your budget for that half a million-dollar business. The rest may come from the bank via that Small Business Administration loan. And any bank whose commercial lender you speak with is going to care about only one thing: ***Can this business reliably pay back the loan?***

Enter a new concept for many of you, called **DSCR**, or **Debt Service Coverage Ratio**. Very simply, it goes like so, with two numbers in a fraction, or the ratio:

- **Numerator**—the business's free cashflow from operations (what the bank calls "net operating income")
- **Denominator**—the monthly loan payment

If the business has enough cushion—enough coverage—you're in much better shape. If the deal is tight, you're living on the bleeding edge and probably ought not be.

Now, are there actually government rules pertaining to any of this? There is! The bare-minimum DSCR is 1.15 times under common SBA small-business acquisition loan guidelines, meaning cash flow must cover debt payments plus at least 15 percent. The technical term for that is . . . "cushion."

What most lenders aim for in practice, however, is 1.25 times or higher. This is the widely cited target and commonly referenced minimum for standard approvals, especially for business acquisitions, working capital, or equipment. A 1.25 times DSCR means the business generates 25 percent more cash flow than needed to cover the debt, creating a buffer for fluctuations. Some lenders may require 1.3 times to 1.5 times (or even higher!) for riskier deals, startups, or certain industries. Like beauty, risk is in the eye of the beholder. Unfortunately, that beholder is not you. You are the beholden.

My rule is as follows: If you're not liquid enough to keep the business running for six months without taking a salary, keep DSCR above 1.3 times. But if you do have enough liquidity to cover that, going down to 1.15 times to 1.25 times can be acceptable. Just know that it comes with additional heartburn if you ever have to tap savings or a credit line. This is ultimately a personal "What's my acceptable risk level?" decision. To what extent are you willing to be pageantly scrutinized?

I am personally more conservative, so I prefer to spend more time saying "no" to companies until I get a deal structure that gives me 1.3 times or better DSCR.

Zooming back out now, you obviously want the loan payment to work on paper, absolutely, but you also want it to work when the business hits turbulence.

And you can. Cushion. So, how do you get the money, the right money, that when all's added up you have a favorable ratio? Outside investors and business banking loans will be how, most likely, and with a little help from your new friend the seller. Then and only then . . . the SBA.

But before you start shopping listings, you're going to want to get prequalified. Here's how.

HOW TO GET PREQUALIFIED FOR A BUSINESS LOAN

This is the second and now decreasingly rare instance where business meets real estate. A business purchase loan is like a mortgage.

If you're going SBA, my strong opinion is to **find an SBA Preferred Lender**. Many banks, credit unions, and other financial institutions like certain creditors "do SBA," but if they aren't *officially* preferred, they're winging it. They package it, send it to the SBA, the SBA reviews it, kicks it back, you revise it, you lose time. Don't.

A preferred lender can move far faster because the SBA trusts their process. You can look this up as it's public information:

- How many SBA loans does a given bank do?
- What size of purchases do they specialize in?

Some lenders only do small loans under a quarter-million. Some prefer large loans into the eight figures. Some can pair SBA with additional loans, if you go over SBA caps (yes, there's a maximum, which you're unlikely to hit with this being most of your's first business purchase but just be aware).

As for me, I use First Internet Bank. They're a preferred lender, and my guy there—Alan—is one of the top SBA lenders in the country. I've done multiple deals with him. The process with them or most SBA preferred lenders is straightforward:

- You call the SBA department; get the contact at www.sba.gov.
    - Say:, "I want to get prequalified. I'm looking to buy a business. I want a prequalification letter."
- They're going to ask you about:
    - your background
    - your income history
    - your personal financial statement (assets, liabilities, etc.)
    - tax returns
    - credit score

    - what you're trying to buy (at a high level)
- But what they're really asking is . . .
    - Are you a person worth lending to?
- If you have decent credit (mid-to-upper 600s and above), a reasonable income history, and you're serious, you can often get a prequal. letter that says, essentially . . .
    - "If the deal makes sense, we would lend up to $###,###."
    - Most times, that number will be the maximum; the bank can't underwrite any specific business yet because they don't know the cashflow and the details. They're just telegraphing, *Would we lend to you in the right circumstances? Yes, these* . . . It's called "prequalification," remember?
- Said letter then becomes part of your buyer package when you start talking to brokers and sellers.

What an SBA Loan Actually Is

With an SBA loan, the SBA is not actually the lender. It turns out, there are three parties:

- You (the borrower)
- The bank (the lender supplying the funds)
- The SBA (the insurer)

If the loan goes bad, the SBA pays the bank back up to a portion—often up to 75 percent of the loan amount. So on a $1,000,000 loan, the bank might get $750,000 back from the SBA if things go sideways.

Your personal guarantee is still real. Now the SBA has paid out. But the SBA—the government—is going to come look for its money. Like I said, they can look at your assets, your 401(k), your checking and savings, your income. They can garnish wages.

The reason this program exists is because it's meant to help people who are capable—but not ultra-wealthy—buy small businesses and keep them alive. There's even a net worth limit for eligibility; if your net worth is too high, you don't qualify.

I fully support this. Finally, the government is doing something right. The SBA is essentially making it possible for normal people to do these deals by limiting the bank's downside—because otherwise the bank would never lend that much money for that long at those rates.

Alternatives to SBA: Conventional Commercial Loans

You should know about these just in case with the SBA loan added in, you're still not quite to the 100 percent of the money you need for your price range (and geography and industry). There are normal commercial loans that sometimes have different terms and sometimes can be non-personally guaranteed. Typically, they're shorter duration—five years is common—which means higher monthly payments. Breaking down the trade-off real quick . . .

- Potential upside: maybe better interest rate, maybe less personal guarantee exposure
- Real downside: higher monthly payment, less flexibility, tighter cashflow risk

And again, small business cashflow is not a straight line, so you have to decide what kind of risk you want to carry. A bank, for a normal commercial loan, is going to more strictly scrutinize your direct industry experience as a borrower. This could, without a cosigner, make it more difficult to get this loan out of the gate. Often, if it makes sense, buyers will go with an SBA loan first, then refinance into another type of loan after they already own the company—but only if the commercial loan rate and terms are more appealing but they had trouble out of the gate getting one to purchase the business. Personally, here's where I land on all this . . .

I'm not telling you to always do SBA; I'm telling you to stop making this emotional and start making it structured. Don't assume paying cash is safer, don't assume a bigger down payment is automatically smarter, don't assume seller financing solves your equity injection problem anymore, and don't assume investors are going to want to be angels and give you 70 to 80 percent of what you need (if they catch wind of any SBA loan for the rest, they're out at that point).

But *do* get prequalified early and know what a bank will actually support. And once you understand your funding path, you're ready for the next "pitch," as it were. See, no one knows who you are, most likely; no one with a potentially-ideal business for you knows why they should do a deal with you. So that's where we go next—how to sell yourself as a buyer.

CHAPTER 7

How to Be the Best Buyer Without the Best Offer

THE HARDEST PART OF BUYING A BUSINESS IS finding the right deal.

Right?

Wrong!

In my and other buyers' experience—once you meet one, you meet hundreds; birds of a feather—**the hardest part of buying a business for a first-time buyer is selling yourself and your offer to the seller**.

Now, your approach will depend on, well, your approach! Are you going through a **broker**? Or are you going directly to the seller on an **off-market deal**?

Obviously, the pitch will be different. I'll show you. Either way, get it right, and you can be the best potential buyer—even if you're *not* the highest offer. But you're still the best. And it starts with a résumé letter. This is a standard document, a one-page letter, that effectively says in four to five paragraphs, "Here's why you should sell your business to me."

Your specifics will depend, again, on your approach. **If it's a broker listing**—something you found on BizBuySell or a similar marketplace—you don't know the seller yet, so a lot of the details are anonymous. So what are you really doing in that first reach-out? You're selling yourself as a *serious* buyer. Consider phrases like:

- "I'm a professional looking to buy a business in this industry."
- "I'm looking for this type of business in this geography."
- "I'm pre-qualified to buy; here's my pre-qualified letter."
- "I'd like more information. Is there a Non-Disclosure Agreement I can sign so we can discuss the business?"

You won't know anything else yet. You might have rough geography, the industry, and some high-level financials, but you don't know the seller and the real story, and you're not going to learn any detailed financials until you're under that NDA.

In reply, the broker might ask some follow-up questions that all basically translate to, "Do you know what the f— you are doing?" This is not the time to panic *à la* the Chapter 5 opening. A way to skip right over that objection is to demonstrate seriousness and commitment to geography and industry with this line in either your opening (often called executive) summary or your cover letter or both: "I'm specifically interested in a plumbing business in central South Carolina" There aren't that many plumbing businesses for sale in one area at one time. So being specific signals credibility because you've narrowed it down so far that it's basically them and two other people (not literally, but directionally).

Now, **if you're going direct to the seller (off-market)**, make it personal as early as possible. Go to the website. Look at Google reviews. Read a few. Then say something specific in your very first message, like "I really admire your business because . . ." and, "I saw that a customer said this about your business, and that's exactly what I'm looking for . . ."

That minute detail works wonders. It tells them you're not mass-spamming a hundred owners. It tells them you actually looked at their business. The sooner you can have that kind of conversation, the more believable you are as a buyer.

You'll need that rapport because your offer may not be the best financially. Here's how to handle that issue, in advance.

HOW TO WIN WHEN YOU'RE NOT THE HIGHEST OFFER

Sellers (and brokers) love to say, "We have other interested buyers." Sometimes it's true. Sometimes it's a lie. But there's no downside for them saying it, same as in real estate, "We've got a lot of interest in this house." It may be false, but assume you're competing. Now, if you're competing against private equity or a roll-up buyer—someone who is likely to outbid you—you need to compete on a different plane. Even in your initial pitch, be direct and say something akin to, "I'm not an institutional buyer. I'm interested in owning and running this business." Then once you're under NDA and you know the particulars . . . you can get a lot more personal.

A seller will usually give you a CIM—confidential information memorandum. How they sell their business in that CIM informs you what they think *you* care about. But it might also tell you what *they* are most proud of in their business. So pay attention. Then tailor your deal—that is, your pitch—to what they're already telling you.

For example, in my first deal, the sellers leaned heavily on the fact that they had a young guy (they volunteered he was thirty years old) who was "the president in waiting." That one detail told me multiple things, specifically:

- They think I'm going to want to know there's someone capable to run the business (e.g. they think I may be an absentee owner or private equity)
- I have to make this kid happy; he's a key employee I don't want to lose.
- They're proud of him, and the company respects him.

Now I can compete differently as a buyer.

How Private Equity Can't Beat You

In that deal, I had four private equity firms competing with me. The reason I won was because I did very personal things. Continuing my short storyline, I put in writing that, from day one, I intended to make that "president in waiting" an equity partner of at least 10 percent. That told the seller I was serious, I wasn't greedy, and I wouldn't make him feel like a jerk for leaving his guys behind. And now I've got an internal advocate (the "president in waiting" who sees that this deal entails him getting equity).

Meanwhile, private equity is not going to walk in and give 10 percent equity to some barely-thirty-year-old. They might offer bonuses, profit sharing, a vesting schedule, the ability to buy in, something like that. But PE is looking for multiples. Buy at three- or four-times EBITDA, sell at seven-plus within a few years. Giving away meaningful equity, up front, across a roll-up eats into that whole model.

So if you're an individual buyer, you can do things institutional buyers won't do. Different plan, different game.

That said, if PE or some other institutional buyer really wants to outbid you, they can. Their pockets are deep. So your job is to make your deal feel better, make it feel more human, without doing something stupid with the numbers. For instance, PE may come in with a higher headline price but with a more aggressive earn-out, meaning if the business doesn't hit certain numbers over two to four years, the owner doesn't get paid. If you can be less aggressive (but still keep incentives in place) that can be more appealing. You can also make employees happier than PE, like I said, and the seller may genuinely prefer selling to someone who actually wants to run their business, instead of selling to a PE firm from Manhattan or Chicago.

You've taken it from, "Pick the highest number," to, "Let's make a deal we both win on, now and years from now."

The faster you make it personal—and the more you show you're listening to and perceiving what's truly important to the seller—the better off you are. For the third time, this is like selling a house, but the one your kids grew up in. You might take a slightly lower offer from people you like over a slightly if not even substantially higher (10 to 20 percent) offer from people acting like entitled, snooty jerks. That's especially true with a business because it's the workforce-equivalent to a child—it's "my baby."

So while you won't want to say "I will beat anyone's offer" (because that may not be true), say instead something like "My goal is to give you a fair price for what you built—something you can and should be proud of—and I'm going to take care of it afterwards. I really care about your business."

It's their baby; tell them you'll take care of it. And mean it! They may just let you.

CHAPTER 8

Seek, Find, First Contact

AND SO IT BEGINS. THE SEARCH. FOR MOST OF YOU, there are two paths. I recommend walking them both so you'll know you didn't miss whatever the other may have had to offer.

Now, one path is faster and well-built. The other is slower and well, frankly, messier. And that's OK because the payoff can be more rewarding.

Obviously I am referring to on-market versus off-market deals. Let's start our search with the first path.

ON MARKET: Faster Finds, Higher Prices

If you're going on-market, visit several sites, not just one. There are a couple major ones—BizBuySell and Dealstream —where you can sign up, set your geography, price point, minimum SDE, industry, and more. You can also set alerts for businesses that get listed in the future that match your criteria.

You can also check regional and state brokerage sites, not

just the big national marketplaces, like Sunbelt Business Brokers. Sometimes, you'll find ones not listed on the others, but most of the smaller regional ones will list their businesses on the major sites.

A simple opener works for contacting the smaller brokerages. And yes, I recommend doing this *before* you have found an eligible business to inquire about. Simply fill out their contact form or use their company email and state that you're an entrepreneur looking to buy a business in this area. You want to know what kind of inventory they have, and you want to learn more about their brokerage services and what types of businesses they represent. See, it's worth building that relationship early because sometimes they'll have wind of something about to come on the market before it hits the public sites. Any legal advantage you can get, take.

Pros and Cons of Business Brokers

Everything in life and in business has tradeoffs. Those of the brokerage are stark. On the pluses, brokers help create structure and offer speed. A broker is usually sitting down with the seller and getting basic answers you need—total revenue, SDE or EBITDA, and asking price (even if it isn't publicly listed). They're also often helping the seller package what you need as a buyer, which can make your search faster and more organized.

That said, competition and incentives are major downsides. A broker listing is being widely publicized. More buyers see it. More buyers bid. Price goes up. Not ideal. It's also really easy to become a business broker, so there are bad apples—people who don't know what they're doing, have never sold a business, don't know how to price it, and can actually make it harder to buy a business. If the gist you collect from a local or regional broker site is "I usually do real estate but my friend is selling this business so I'm the listing broker," avoid. Regardless of competence, the broker is taking 8 to 12 percent of the sale price. The seller pays it, not the buyer, but it's baked into the price—like real estate (sorry; this analogy works more often than it doesn't). Broker psychology is the same as a real estate agent. The more people there are who want to get a cut, the greater the incentive for all parties to work against you as the buyer; everyone wants it to look clean and dressed up, and it's often inflated. No moral judgments from me, just incentives. But there is another way.

OFF MARKET: Slower Deals, Better Terms

Off-market sales are going to be slower and more hands-on. Often, you're the one who reaches out. They "could sell, could not sell," you'll probably hear verbatim, and they may not have even made up their mind yet. So you're not only educating them on how a sale goes, you're also selling them on the idea that, yes, they actually should sell their business. And not just to you . . . to anyone!

That said, the cons of buying from a brokerage are the pros of seeking deals off market. Less competition, lower multiples, no cut-taking middlemen, more flexibility in the deal. But are they messier? Yes, and that's *not* a con of buying direct. Messy is good. A feature not a bug. It's like a staged property versus a "sorry, we didn't have time to clean up" house that's actually lived in. See, on-market can feel similarly . . . "staged." Off-market is more like seeing what it's actually like day-to-day. What are you buying versus what would a broker be financially incentivized to convince you that you are buying? Two different answers most of the time.

Messy also means you can quickly learn how much of this "business" is actually the owner's *job*. And because there's not a professional deceiver assisting them (again, incentives!), you get a clearer view of reality earlier. Messy reality is the default off market; staged illusions are the default on market. In any system where money talks, it will scream over the quiet fine print.

Fear Not Greed

There's an interesting dynamic when reaching out to off-market buyers. Many haven't decided whether or not they are sellers at all! See, many buyers assume the owner will get greedy. In my experience, off-market is more often fear, not greed. They're afraid they're getting taken advantage of—signing bad contracts, not knowing what they're doing, dealing with some shyster buying their business for pennies on the dollar because they don't know better.

That means your posture matters. You are part rescuer, helper, organizer, teacher, part "adult supervision." Anything you tell them, they will pass right on to their accountant, then their tax attorney (if they have one), then their business lawyer (which of course they are going to hire next, followed by a professional business valuation consultant). Often, the owner will put you directly in touch with their accountant—after a very reasonable nondisclosure agreement is signed, of course. But once you're talking to the business owner's accountant, you can have a reasonable conversation to learn what you need to—what multiples businesses like this go for, what true EBITDA really is, and how to structure a deal that's tax-beneficial for the seller (asset sale versus equity sale, S-corp vs C-corp dynamics, etc.).

I'll straight-up tell owners to get a business lawyer, by the way; I even recommend an M&A lawyer. It reassures them I'm not trying to hide anything, and the right professional will protect both sides. But what they do not need is a broker to take a cut.

Finding Off-Market Sellers

Off-market is all relationships, so it's slower. There are no ready-made listings as with a broker. Sometimes you put feelers out there and get no action for six to nine months. You're looking one at a time for businesses, and there can be no obvious red flags. Usual places I look include:

- Secretary of State lists (especially for licensed trades)
    - In one case, I pulled all commercial electrical contractors from North Carolina's Secretary of State listings, identified the master electrician or licensed person associated with each company, and got contact info that way.
- Local business journals (top 100 lists by industry/region)
- M&A lawyers and tax accountants who work with small and medium-sized businesses
    - A handful of these people often touch most of the reasonable-size businesses in a niche. If you build real relationships here, they can become deal fountains.
- The business' own contact form or web page
    - Does the business have a Gmail or other free email service provider? This is a "tell" that the business may not be big enough to buy. Do they have their own domain name-based email? Better.

Now, this is not baseball where you need to hit .300. Here, you don't need many wins. If a hundred people know what you're looking for, and one works out, that's millions and millions of dollars in your pocket.

For outreach, I've done this—build a simple site explaining who you are and what you're doing, then send emails from that domain and link to the site so they can check you out. It's basically just an "about page" for you as a business professional, but the home page of the website. Some call these personal-brand websites. You should have it for your career outside entrepreneurship regardless. Anyway, email marketing tools like Hubspot allow you to see who clicked a link in your email. Now you've got signal. *This guy looked.*

Personally, I looked at dozens of businesses—electrical contractors in my geography. I hired a part-time virtual assistant at $15 an hour to cold-call my entire list and follow up with email, then call again a couple weeks later with a simple script. Something like, "We're looking for great electrical companies in your area; have you ever thought about selling?" This person's job is just to sort interested versus not interested and build a warm lead list for me to call personally. I recommend doing the same.

Now, people get a billion emails and assume it's automated. Phone calls, in my experience, have a pretty good success rate. But do both. The email link-click is what you want to know; just that one action indicates potential interest in selling their business—or at least learning more about the person (you) who may want to buy it.

Once you've got your warm leads list—they told your assistant they are willing to entertain a conversation with you—personally call yourself. Then keep it simple. Offer lunch and ask if they'd be willing to talk. Some will say no. That's fine. I typically say, "No problem. I'm going to send a follow-up email so you have my information. If you change your mind, I'm around." Then, make yourself a note to follow up in three to six months—three if they seemed interested at all, six if they seemed cooled-off to the idea at first. And when you do, revisit where you left off as they may have forgotten. Two to three sentences, tops, should do it.

NDA Before Anything

Off-market owners can be skittish because they don't want people to know they're even talking about selling. So I'll offer NDA early—often before they divulge much of anything—because even the fact they're discussing a sale could damage the business if employees or customers catch wind of it. I'll say something like, "If you want, we can do an NDA between the two of us; anything you tell me stays between us. I can send one, or if you have one, I'm happy to sign it.

That first serious (usually in-person) conversation is probably not the time for deep financials. This meeting is really a culture fit and vibe check. If you're going to take over caregiving for their "baby," the relationship dynamic itself matters.

RUN THE NUMBERS

Once there is an NDA in place, it's time to get a few financials from their accountant. This is specifically for the off-market owners, but you'll run the numbers *before* contacting a brokerage about any one specific business listing. You need to know if the math checks out before any serious further engagement with that particular business.

Fortunately, there's a spreadsheet for that, and you can download it on my website.

bluebacks.co/cashflow

You'll ask for the specific financials listed in this spreadsheet template from the off-market owner's accountant once you're under NDA. You need no such conversations prior to running the numbers with a brokerage website, however.

So what, exactly, is this spreadsheet and why should you use it—before issuing an **Indication of Interest letter (IOI)** to the brokerage? (That's where you basically say, "I like what I see initially, so here is my first offer, my terms, my ability to run, proof I can buy it via my preapproval," etc.) Because you'll be a bit deeper into the business with an off-market owner, what with the NDA and all, you don't really need an IOI; you can skip right to the **Letter of Intent (LOI)**, which is what we'll be covering together in Chapter 8. If the brokerage responds positively to your IOI, *then* you will write an LOI.

OK, back to the spreadsheet to run the numbers to confirm you want to make an offer in the first place!

The template you'll be downloading is not a substitute for diligence, a Quality of Earnings (which you'll pay for after the LOI), or what your banker will require later. It is, however, a first-pass filter that answers this question:

> If I bought this business on reasonable terms, would it produce enough cash flow to survive and be worth my time?

It forces reality early—especially around debt service, owner earnings, and how thin the margin for error can get once you layer financing on top of a business.

Besides the **Instructions** tab in the spreadsheet download, you'll see a **Key Assumptions** tab. This is where you define the deal at a high level—what you're buying, what you're paying, and how you're financing it. You'll input things like:

- Net purchase price (what the seller receives for the business)
- Growth "overfund" (extra SBA loan dollars earmarked for integration/growth costs, optional)
- Acquisition support costs (legal, accounting, diligence, closing costs . . . real cash that's easy to forget)
- Revenue, gross profit, and TTM SDE (so the model knows what it's working with)

Then you set up the financing mix:

- SBA loan amount (and it calculates fees)
- Seller financing amount

- Buyer equity (your cash in)
- Optional minority investor assumptions (if applicable)

Next, the loan terms (actual if you already know or close enough if you don't):

- SBA term and interest rate
- Seller financing term and interest rate

From those, the model calculates monthly payments and gives you a quick DSCR view, your lender's favorite acronym. D*oes the business produce enough earnings to cover debt payments with a buffer?* If DSCR is weak in this projection, it's not going to magically become strong later.

There is one more tab in the free spreadsheet, the **Cash Flow Model**. Here, you'll be forecasting what the business looks like after purchase:

- Revenue and revenue growth by year
- Gross margin and gross margin changes
- Operating expense assumptions
- Adjusted EBITDA / SDE
- Total debt payments (SBA and seller note)
- DSCR targets (the model gives you a sanity nudge; try to keep it above approx. 1.5)
- A build cash float / maintenance CAPEX line item (real businesses break things and require cash)

Because it's a set of formulas you can enter different numbers into, the spreadsheet lets you run scenarios. For example, you can force answers for the questions of risk, like:

- What happens if revenue falls but gross profit improves?

- What happens if you invest more in marketing?
- What happens if you need additional headcount to support growth?

That tab also includes a simple exit multiple section so you can see what the business might be worth later, net of remaining debt. Now, that's not the main reason you buy a business like this (that's the PE job), but it's still helpful to see how the story ends if you execute well.

From the above formulas, you'll come away with one of three answers for any business you vet before the IOI or LOI:

INSTANT NO

The deal can't support debt. The cash flow collapses. DSCR looks ugly. Move on.

MAYBE

It's close. Depends on price, structure, seller note terms, or if earnings are really real. Still useful. Tells you what questions to ask next.

YES, WORTH PURSUING

Debt is serviceable. Post-debt cash flow is real. There's margin for error. Now you've earned the right to contact the broker. Or, off-market, to take the next serious meeting and begin discussing terms.

And now you're ready. Assuming you've found a couple of businesses that fit your criteria, don't display any red flags, and don't prove to be *Instant No* based on your handy spreadsheet tool, we're going to take this relationship itself off the market. Here's what happens next.

CHAPTER 9

Letter of Intent, the Exclusivity Period, and Quality of Earnings

THIS IS IT. YOU'VE GOT A LIVE ONE. IT'S TIME TO make your offer.

. . . assuming you see *no* red flags. *No* rules broken. Is that the case? This book is recursive now. Go back to Chapter 4. You have more data now with an NDA in place, real financial data. The good stuff. And you're about to get more. But before you drop approximately $20,000 on outside experts for the next stage of the buying journey, confirm that there will, in fact, be a next stage.

If you see *any* red flag or *any* rule gets broken, you don't push through, rationalize, or tell yourself you'll fix it later. You walk.

Otherwise, run it by your lender. You'll basically say, "This is what I'm looking at. This is how I'm thinking about structuring it. What do you think?" This is a sanity check, and it's free. They'll need to agree anyway to get the deal done.

Alright then. No red flags? All rules good? In that case—and assuming you've punched in your newest, most up-to-date financial data from the business in question into that handy spreadsheet to show that the math indeed checks out—the biz is effectively vetted into the next stage.

LOI: Like a House Under Contingent Sale

The further we get into this book, the more alike business acquisition seems to be to real estate. In any case, the Letter of Intent (LOI) is similar to the state of a property in sale-pending status. The sale is contingent. There's an offer, and it's accepted, but closing has not yet occurred. In dating terms, you're engaged to be married, and you're off the market now. But you can still walk away relatively easily, logistically speaking.

So again, assuming no red flags and a financial model that works, you're going to write and submit a Letter of Intent. Right now, your goal as the likely buyer is simply to get the seller to stop shopping the company to other buyers. Putting it informally, your LOI is basically you communicating, *Based on what I know right now, I'm in. Here's what I intend to pay. Here's how I intend to structure it. Now I need time to prove what you told me is true. And because that vetting is going to cost me real money, I need you to stop talking to other buyers during that period.*

And there's the rub of contingency; it's an if/then-style statement. *As in, If what you've told me is true—if the business is what you've represented—then I'm valuing your business at this, and I'm prepared to move forward.*

But to justify the money you're about to spend proving your hypothesis, you need exclusivity.

WHAT GOES IN THE LETTER OF INTENT

I've noticed in aspiring entrepreneurial circles it's believed that the LOI is "the price" you are going to "agree" on. That's partially true, but it's not the most important aspect. The LOI is where you make the seller feel, *This is real. This buyer is serious and has thought it through.*

Yes, you do include the purchase price. But you also include the structure, i.e.,:

- What portion is upfront cash?
- What portion is a seller note?
- What portion is earnouts?
- What portion is tied to future performance?

All this is to be included because you're (probably) not borrowing 100 percent from the bank or just dropping a bag of cash on the table. That's not how most deals work. Most deals consist of structure and incentive alignment. You want the owner to get paid, but you also want the structure to protect you and the business after closing. After close, you're walking into a living organism—employees, customers, vendors, relationships, culture, reputation. You don't want a structure that leaves you with zero oxygen and maximum pressure the day after you take the keys.

Beyond structure, the LOI is also where you put in anything else that's material—anything that matters to the seller—because this is where you're selling yourself and your offer to them. For instance, you might upfront-commit to making a key employee a true partner—with real equity—as I did. I wanted that in writing early to ease the seller's mind, to protect this particular superstar of a worker in the new business structure. Everyone feels good about that.

One more time—you can still walk away. You are not locked

in. But the more specific you are in your offer, your LOI, the more seriously the seller will take you. And potentially, the more easily they may work with you negotiationwise.

Besides employees, get into the specifics of what's in it for the seller personally. This is more than a numbers game. Consider, for example, do they want to retire clean? Do they want to keep a role? Do they want a transition? Do they want a legacy? Do they want their people taken care of? Do they want certainty? Do they want the maximum headline price?

In some deals, these considerations may lead you to include a real salary for the seller to keep working during transition. As an aside, I'm negotiating a(nother) deal right now where I'm going to offer a $300,000 annual salary to incentivize the soon-to-be-previous owner to keep working. Specificity reduces fear. It also distinguishes you from tire-kickers.

Obviously it will take some time to think through all of this. It's worth it. To you both. Obviously. Because remember what you're asking the seller to do—to take the business off the market. That costs them. They're saying no to any other potential conversations while they give you the time to vet the business. So your offer has to be serious. This is an exclusivity period. Use it wisely.

THE QUALITY OF EARNINGS REPORT

Once you have an LOI and you've got that sweet exclusivity, you're entering the period where you take the business apart and see what's actually inside it. This is where the Quality of Earnings report comes in to either change everything, or confirm it. Think of it like an appraisal for a bank buying a home (sorry, real estate again, not sorry). Except the house is a business, and the foundation is cash flow.

If you're financing the deal, which almost every one of you will, the bank is going to require a third-party Quality of Earnings report. These typically take forty-five to sixty days to deliver. The QOE firm you hire will ask for a pile of documents from the business in question, such as:

- bank statements
- tax information
- financial reports
- supporting schedules
- other detail-laden documentation behind the numbers

When all's said and done, they're going to tell you whether the earnings you're basing your valuation on are real, stable, and supported. They'll find discrepancies, yes—but they'll also find "non-discrepancy problems." These might include earnings overly concentrated in one customer, earnings that are highly variable year to year, or earnings that look fine on average but are unstable in reality. So you might have a three-year average EBITDA of $3 million, but if two years were $500,000 and one year was between $6 and $7 million, that's a completely different risk profile than a stable $3 million year after year. The QOE brings to your attention any such stability—or total lack thereof. It also helps you see what's forward-looking, if you ask them to. As an example, in the construction industry, that means things like:

- jobs / work in progress
- project backlog
- budgets versus actual expenses
- new opportunities under contract

Think of it like this. A QOE is a lot like an appraiser. They'll tell you if something is catastrophically wrong. They'll tell you if the foundation is cracked. They'll tell you if the earnings are fake. But if the business is more or less worth what you're offering, they'll generally confirm that the data supports it. Expect to spend a minimum of $7,000 on the QOE, by the way. More if it's a complicated business that needs very specific expertise.

Now, assuming the QOE report is acceptable and no hidden red flags appear, you'll proceed to hiring a mergers and acquisitions (M&A) lawyer who will review the *offer* with you. This is the actual legal contract that comes next when it's time to move forward. So, get this person in place to confirm no funny business. This will set you back about $7,000 minimum.

Now, that's useful, but it's not enough. If you're really smart—and you are, because you decided to read this book—you'll also hire a second person who isn't writing a report for the bank. Someone who is just for you. Who will poke holes. Who'll play the pessimist and say, in as many words, "If I were betting the house, how could this fail?"

This individual might be a forensic accountant, an investor, a serial entrepreneur you know, or a business lawyer known for prophesying doom and being uncannily accurate. There isn't one perfect role to find to fill the professional pessimist's job; I call it the *consigliere*. They have no incentive to lie to you, and they aren't worried about what their advice will look like to the bank or the seller. You'll probably pay this person somewhere around $2,000 regardless of their profession.

And now, you're ready. I mean, *really* ready.

DECIDING

This decision should be boring, actually. Your process should have done its job for you. The decision criteria is basically:

- No unexplained red flags
- The financial model works
- Worst-case scenarios still work
- Your risk tolerance is respected
- You can't prove yourself "no"

This is also where you go back to the spreadsheet and run the numbers yet again. So plug it all in, test assumptions, and stress-test the deal. Does the cash flow work? Not in the best case but in the worst case.

If the deal still meets your criteria, you make the offer, you write the LOI, and you move into due diligence.

But first, there are a couple side issues that may distract from the main quest at this juncture. Let's discuss.

MANAGING EMOTIONS: Yours and Theirs

A business is the biggest purchase most people will ever make. There will be big emotions. There will be fear. There will be spikes of adrenaline and doubt. And you'll be managing two people's emotions: yours and the seller's.

During the LOI-to-close window, you'll ask the seller for a lot of documents. You'll ask questions that feel intrusive. You'll bring in third parties who will poke around. Remember, he's selling his baby. Your job becomes keeping him calm, keeping him even-keeled, reassuring him. You'll be a part-time therapist. Every problem that comes up is just another item to check off the list. *Negative thing appears? Great. Now it's on the list. What would need to be proven to me for this to not be a problem? What do I need to see? What questions need answers?*

Then you do it one at a time. As long as you keep doing that, you keep marching toward the finish line. Now, that finish line might be "yes," or it might be "no." Either way, you're moving forward. No panic, all process.

When someone has never been through this before, anything big that pops up looks like a deal-breaker at first glance or glimpse. People react emotionally . . . throw their hands up . . . say, "I'm out; forget it."

No. Wait. The right move is almost always to take a mental and emotional step back. *What would have to be true for this to still work?* Write down the questions. Then go find the expert who can answer them. You may oscillate between *absolutely no* and *hell yeah!* several times during the exclusivity period. You may even do so on the same day—multiple times.

I'm living this right now at the time of this writing with a partner who has never gone through an acquisition before. We're looking at a company that's a union shop. If you go online, you'll find a thousand reasons it's complicated. And my partner's reaction was, "I'm a thousand percent out," upon hearing the news.

My response was simple: If we're going to say no, we're going to say no for explicable, rational reasons we can explain. Not for fear. So, we'll keep walking down the path until we reach a question we can't answer satisfactorily. Then do we walk away? Or do we answer it and realize it wasn't a problem all along?

But there might be problems that are very real even if they aren't about the business—they're about the seller. These are rarer but still worth covering as we close out.

MID-SALE ANTICS TO BE AWARE OF

Certain seller behaviors should make you leery. Pay attention to them, especially post-LOI, mid-sale, when details start tightening. Here's a common one—the seller keeps trying to renegotiate the seller note.

Now, most seller notes are about incentive alignment. The idea is that if the business performs post-close, the seller gets paid; if it doesn't, they don't get the full amount. For example, say they get $2 million if EBITDA hits $###,### over the next two years and they get another $2 million if it hits $#,###,###. That keeps everyone honest. But suppose the seller starts pushing to lower the threshold—especially repeatedly—that's information. Let's say that at first, the threshold is $5 million. Then they want $4 million. Then $3. Then they want pro rata so they get paid even if performance drops below the threshold.

> Why are you worried about performance below $4 million if you haven't been below $4 million for five years?

Two explanations can both be plausible:

1. He's just conservative. He likes to wheel and deal. This is his last big sale, so he's pushing.
2. He's misrepresenting earnings, or he's afraid future earnings are going to fall off.

I'm seeing red either way, and I'm getting on the phone.

"I want to understand. Are earnings falling off a cliff? Is revenue declining? Because you're asking for protection below a level your books haven't touched in years."

Bla, bla, bla, I hear in response. OK. I lay down my boundary.

"Fine. I'll put pro rata in the LOI if you want. But just know what happens next. I'm going to really scrutinize your forward-looking earnings—works in progress, backlog, everything—much harder than I would have. And if it doesn't support the EBITDA you're claiming, we're renegotiating price."

If the seller says, "No, you won't find anything," you've cataloged a very important data point. If he also casually mentions, "Yeah, work's been slowing a little bit," that's another data point.

Now you've got multiple signals pointing in the same direction—the seller pushing thresholds down, comments about slowing work, and unusual anxiety about future performance. Interesting. Your strategy now becomes intense forward-looking revenue scrutiny. Alert your experts; insist they return to you with the truth. So now you can speak with it.

"The original purchase price doesn't make sense given forward-looking earnings. We need to reduce price, or I'm walking."

Look, anyone with millions of dollars on the table is going to do what he's doing—protect his investment. He can shop it around if he wants, but the next serious buyer will find the same things. And if he isn't willing to fairly value the business based on what's real, you move forward to a "no." But again, you're still moving forward.

The seller has more to lose from you walking away. But you have more to lose by proceeding when you shouldn't.

There is going to be a win-win, or a win-lose—only if you are prepared to walk and win the next opportunity to check out another business. But you throw the seller a win-lose in his direction if you skip anything in this chapter. Don't.

CHAPTER 10

The Purchase Agreement

WE CLOSED OUT CHAPTER 8 WITH THE PRACTICAL reminder to hold all the cards, to maintain your power in the negotiation. I don't believe it's possible to under-sell how important this is. That's what shrewd but likely-unethical sellers will try to get you to show your cards and give away your power at every point in the courtship that is business acquisition. One way I didn't mention in Chapter 8 that some sellers will do this is they will attempt to get you to skip Chapter 8 almost entirely and come right down to the material here in Chapter 9.

> We don't need to do an LOI; let's just get right to a bare-bones purchase agreement. That's plenty. You'll see. We'll save you time, and we can just add whatever contingencies . . .

Unless it's, for example, your own father who owns the business you're buying, don't do this. No step-skipping. Sketchy sellers want you to skip due diligence because they themselves are suspect, and they know what you're likely to find during the exclusivity period, particularly when the QOE report comes back.

And now we're back to the real estate analogy. Would you buy a property without an inspection? I can think of very few circumstances where I would. Where anyone would! There's a reason they are trying to rush you, and it's not going to be in your best interest. The LOI exists for a reason. The LOI is that bare bones, high level, "what are we doing here" document. It's how you get under contract enough to justify spending real money on due diligence. If you let them drag you into the purchase agreement too early, you're doing it backward.

Here's the first problem: it forces you to incur significant legal costs before you've even completed due diligence. A purchase agreement includes a lot of things an LOI won't. For example, it's going to include indemnities and warranties and a bunch of things that are not needed for an LOI. You're going to incur legal costs drafting all that language before you've actually even gone through diligence. That makes no sense. Because now you're paying for due diligence and paying for the legal costs at the same time. You're stacking costs up front on yourself before you've learned the truth.

And there's a psychological angle here, too—one brokers understand, and some sellers will absolutely use (against you). They're counting on deal momentum; they're counting on sunk cost fallacy. They want you thinking, *I've spent so much money and time doing this already* . . . so you're less likely to walk away. That flips the entire power balance. So instead of *"I will only go forward if . . ."* it becomes *"I will only walk away if . . ."* and that's exactly where you can get hurt.

Now, here's the second problem; LOI-skipping forces you to work with that bare-bones purchase agreement instead of one that actually incorporates the aspects of the deal and the targets and the things you find out in diligence. If you haven't done a Quality of

Earnings yet, if you haven't really validated what's going on, what you discover can change what needs to go into the purchase agreement. That's why doing the purchase agreement first is getting the cart before the horse.

So, if you do this right, Chapter 9 does indeed follow Chapter 8. That said, when is it actually time for Chapter 9? How do you know? Let's talk about it.

READY TO PROCEED

You proceed after the LOI, after exclusivity is in place, after confidentiality is handled, after you've paid for the QOE process and lived through the early parts of diligence.

At that point the question becomes simple: *Did I find anything in due diligence?* And if you're financing the deal—especially with an SBA loan—understand something. The bank is going to have a lot of paperwork they want before you proceed, and it always takes longer than everyone thinks. Even when "everything is approved," the bank will ask for more at the last second. If you roll into a new month or a new quarter, they'll want the most recent numbers, too. That takes time. It goes back to the underwriter. That can take another week. So plan for it. Assume it. Don't panic when it happens. It probably will. And amid it all . . .

GET AN M&A LAWYER

Do not do this with a template. Hire an actual M&A lawyer to draft your purchase agreement. Once you've done the LOI, once you've done enough diligence to know the deal structure makes sense, then you draft the purchase agreement. Or rather, have your attorney do it, which costs money. And that's exactly why you don't want to do it up front.

Now, from here, expect the normal back-and-forth: you send it, they have their lawyer, you have redlines, and there will be a lot of language negotiations—indemnities, exemptions, warranties, non-competes, transition language, the stuff that wasn't in your LOI beyond high-level terms. There's a lot of it. Let's have a section-by-section preview.

WHAT'S ACTUALLY INSIDE THE PURCHASE AGREEMENT

A purchase agreement is the document that decides, in writing, what you're buying, what you're not buying, who eats what risk, what happens if something's wrong, and what happens if someone lies. It's the playbook-meets-rulebook for the transfer of a living, breathing machine that already has customers, employees, vendors, debt, liabilities, contracts, leases, permits, and unfinished work.

It's also where people accidentally get trapped; once you're paying your M&A attorney to draft and negotiate this thing, those deal momentum and sunk-cost dangers can manifest. That's why I'm so adamant—don't let a broker pull you into a purchase agreement too early. Save the heavy legal lift for when you've earned it through LOI, exclusivity, and early diligence. Then when you're ready, you're ready. And here's what you're ready for—**the contents of a purchase agreement**.

Deal Terms

The purchase agreement spells out whether this is an asset deal or an equity deal, and that choice changes everything. In an asset deal you're usually buying selected assets and leaving a bunch of liabilities behind. In an equity deal you're buying the entity—and with it, the entity's baggage.

Then it locks in the purchase price and the structure, e.g., cash at close, seller note, earn-out, escrow/holdback, and any adjustments. It also defines the "what" of the transaction—inventory, equipment, customer lists, phone numbers, websites, vehicles, tools, works in progress, deposits, intellectual property, and so on.

This section also usually forces the uncomfortable question: *What is actually included in the sale, and what is the seller quietly assuming he gets to keep?* All must be answered. Nothing is left to chance. Good.

Purchase Price Adjustment (and Protection)

Many buyers will learn this one the hard way. It's common for agreements to include a mechanism that adjusts the final purchase price based on something measurable at closing, most often working capital (or "net working capital"). The reason is obvious when I spell it out. If you thought you were buying a business with enough cash/receivables/inventory to operate normally, but you show up at closing and the seller has drained cash, delayed payables, or let receivables rot, you didn't buy what you priced. The working-capital adjustment is meant to prevent that shell game.

Representations and Warranties

Representations and warranties are the seller's statements of fact about the business. Take things like:

- the financial statements are accurate (or at least not misleading)

- taxes were filed and paid
- there are no undisclosed debts
- the business owns what it says it owns
- key contracts are valid and transferable
- there aren't hidden lawsuits, liens, or regulatory problems
- employees are properly classified and paid
- the seller has the authority to sell

Representations and warranties are almost always limited and shaped by "disclosure schedules." In real-world deals, the agreement might say "no litigation"—and then a schedule lists exceptions, like a demand letter here, a threatened claim there, a dispute with a vendor, etc. The reps are not true in the abstract; they're "true except as disclosed."

Covenants

Between signing and closing, a business can change a lot. So the purchasing agreement typically requires the seller to operate "in the ordinary course," not do anything weird, and not make major moves without your consent. This is where you see rules around things like:

- no new debt
- no unusual owner distributions
- no major hires/fires or compensation changes
- no new contracts outside normal practice
- no selling off equipment or "cleaning out the shop"
- keeping insurance in place
- maintaining permits and licenses

If the seller starts acting squirrelly during this period, the covenants are the guardrails. Antics indicate anything *but* an ordinary course of business. Stay alert.

I'll give you a real example on this. A day before closing, a seller went and billed a bunch of customers early—not a standard business operation. Nothing illegal, but it wasn't how the business normally operated. This artificially juiced his receivables, and there was a clause in the contract that I owed him money if receivables exceeded a certain amount. If I hadn't caught it when buying that business (not the commercial electrical contractor, by the way, a different purchase that came later), it would have created a huge liability for me to pay him. But because I did catch it—and because I had language in the contract saying they have to operate according to standard operating procedures between purchase agreement and closing, especially regarding liabilities—I could push back. I handed him the documentation and made it clear I wasn't paying for that maneuver. He relented. He had no choice.

Conditions to Closing

This is one of the most important psychological parts of the agreement. In a properly sequenced deal, the purchase agreement reflects reality. You're moving forward only if certain things are true. That shows up as "conditions to closing," requirements that must be satisfied before you're obligated to wire money. Common conditions include:

- financing approval (if applicable)
- acceptable due diligence results (or no material adverse change)
- required third-party consents (e.g., landlords, key customers, vendors)
- no new litigation or regulatory events

- delivery of specific documents (e.g., assignments, bills of sale, intellectual transfers, lien releases)

Yet another reason skipping the LOI is so dangerous—you end up negotiating all of this (expensively) before you've proven the business is worth it.

Indemnification

Indemnification is the agreement's answer to, *OK, but what if that wasn't true?* If a rep is breached, or a liability appears that should've been disclosed, indemnification is how the buyer tries to get paid back. Deals get extremely specific here because indemnification is rarely unlimited. Most agreements have some mix of:

- caps (a maximum total amount the seller is liable for)
- baskets (a minimum threshold of damages before the buyer can claim)
- survival periods (how long reps last before they expire)
- escrow/holdback (money set aside to fund claims)

There are usually carve-outs where the gloves come off, like for fraud, tax issues, or some other potential and realistic risk. Here, you are literally negotiating the damage model for the next several years of your life. Don't negotiate it away. Don't rush.

Non-Compete, Non-Solicit, and Transition

The business you'll be buying is more than equipment and revenue. You're going to be buying relationships, goodwill, and momentum. Therefore, purchase agreements commonly include restrictions and transition provisions, such as guarantees that . . .

- the seller won't compete for a defined period and geography
- the seller won't solicit employees or customers
- the seller will help with transition (often with defined hours/compensation)

This section may also include introduction plans for key customers/vendors and optional transition services agreements.

TAXES AND PURCHASE PRICE ALLOCATION

In an asset acquisition, you generally need to allocate the purchase price across asset classes (e.g., equipment, inventory, intangibles, goodwill, etc.). That allocation affects taxes for both sides, and the IRS expects consistency. In many applicable asset acquisitions, both parties file Form 8594 to report the allocation under Section 1060.

Closing Mechanics

Finally, the agreement lays out what happens on closing day, like escrow instructions (if there's an escrow agent), wire details and timing, which documents are delivered (e.g., bill of sale, assignments, resignations, lien releases, consents, etc.), and post-closing obligations (e.g., final working capital true-up, filings, notices)

Most closings end up being pretty boring. It's usually emails, signatures, wire confirmations. Sometimes, the date is still "TBD" for a while, because the bank's internal process is still moving. The signing itself when eventually it gets scheduled is usually simple. You either go to a lawyer's office or a mobile notary comes to you. It's like buying a house—a big stack of papers, they tell you what to sign, where to sign.

After that, there's often an escrow or closing law firm involved—someone collects the executed documents, verifies signatures and conditions, receives the wired funds, and then releases funds to the seller once everything is satisfied. They'll also handle the formalities like recording with the Secretary of State that ownership has changed hands. It's all pretty boring till you get the news—the business now belongs to you.

CHAPTER 11

It's Yours Now; Now What?

SUCCESS IN THE FIRST THIRTY DAYS OWNING YOUR new business may seem like a low standard. It is, but it's not. And it goes like this:

Success in the first month means nothing breaks.

That's it. Not a revenue increase or new campaign. Neither a new tech deployment nor a new operations optimization. The business must survive the handoff. It's a low standard, but it's the only standard worth measuring.

Now, in your first month as the new owner, you're no visionary; you're the stabilizer. You're trying to keep the machine running while you learn what the machine actually is. If anything hits the fan, it's going to be on or around day thirty. Unless you get really unlucky with a customer, the first real threat is a key employee you assumed would stay has abruptly decided not to.

Again, expect that near the last day of your first month. But for right now, let's focus on what happens at the very beginning of that month so you can start right.

YOUR FIRST FORTY-EIGHT HOURS

The first forty-eight hours after closing are all about control transition. You need to know where the money is. You need to know how the business pays people. You need to know what can go wrong quickly. And you need to make sure nothing is quietly building in the background that turns into an emergency when you're not looking. Let's get into some specifics.

Bank Accounts, Turnover, and Access

Start with all accounts. You need access to the operating account, payroll account, and any other accounts the business uses. If there are multiple accounts—one for deposits, one for payroll, one for taxes—you need visibility into all of them.

If you do nothing else in the first forty-eight hours, make sure you can see cash moving in and out. Make sure you can approve payments. Make sure you can stop payments if something looks off. Make sure you can make payroll.

The business can survive a messy workflow for a few weeks; it cannot survive missed payroll. While you're doing this, don't disappear from your own bank. Get feedback from your bank all along the process. Any new piece of financial information—pre-LOI, pre-close, during due diligence—send it to them and get their feedback on it. That's going to tell you whether or not they're concerned, and it moves the needle on what you need to do next. Why am I still talking about banking in Chapter 10? Because even after closing, the bank is still your best friend. Keep them in the loop. Don't go silent and assume everything will work itself out.

Closing Out Loose Ends and Preventing Liens

Next, close out the obvious risk points. Lines of credit, vendor accounts, suppliers—anywhere the business can quietly rack up obligations that later come back as a surprise. Again, first forty-eight hours.

One of the fastest ways to walk into an avoidable disaster is to inherit confusion around payables and vendor balances and then find out later that somebody decided to file a lien. This is basic, unglamorous work. It's also how you keep the business from being managed by the chaos you didn't create.

YOUR FIRST TWO TO THREE WEEKS

The first two or three weeks are when you begin learning the subjective, undocumented parts of what you actually bought. Your instinct is going to be to come in with a plan; your real job is to come in with questions. You are now a student. Become an expert in how this particular business actually runs. That doesn't mean you have to know everything instantly. It does mean you have to learn how every major function works well enough to see where the gaps are.

"A Day in the Life"

Have the now-previous owner walk you through a day in the life through every office building, center, room, floor, or whatever commercial spaces your new company has. Ask and get clear answers on every single operation that occurs, including but not limited to:

- What does the full workday actually look like?
- How does the phone ring?
- Who answers?

- What happens next?
- Who schedules?
- Who dispatches?
- Who sells?
- Who does the work?
- Who closes out the job?
- Who invoices?
- Who collects?
- Who handles customer complaints?
- Who handles suppliers?
- Who decides what gets approved?
- Who does payroll?
- Who is the bottleneck?

You're trying to see the business as it really exists, not as it was described in the sale process. As you learn, take notes of everything. Record it. Transcribe it. You might think you'll remember what people told you, but you won't. This business likely didn't come with a complete operations manual, so you'll need all those transcripts.

This first new-owner walkthrough is how you start identifying who you may need to hire, who you may need to replace, and where the business is fragile.

Study Business Development

Once you've got your footing—once you understand the day-to-day—your next steep learning curve is business development. Essential questions to answer in full include:

- What is our sales process?

- Do we know how we're selling?
- How do we get business?
- How do we retain business?
- How do we upsell?

Seek first to understand, not fix. Fixing will come in time. And that time will be pretty soon. I'll give you an example.

FIXING THE CALL VERSUS SELLING THE SYSTEM

Say you buy an HVAC company. You're going to get calls like, "My air conditioning broke." Obvious enough. So, a technician goes out, fixes the AC, and leaves. That might be a few hundred dollars, or a thousand dollars—whatever it is. But if that's all that happens, your "sales process" is basically that you rely exclusively on inbound leads, usually SEO, and often pay-per-click. All this, you find when you look into where those calls are coming from. Now, that's not inherently wrong. But are your techs actually selling while they're there? Or are they just responding to calls?

If your technician's mindset is, *I'm just here to fix what's broken,* you're leaving money on the table. What if the right move isn't a $500 repair? What if it's a full replacement? e.g., "Actually, this is a twenty-year-old HVAC system. I can fix it for $500, but you might want a new one."

Let's say our hypothetical HVAC company also provides plumbing services. Now the technician is already in the home. Do you have standard operating procedures that say to check other things we do while we're here? For example, check the water heater. Don't charge the customer to check it. Just look at it. See whether it's out of warranty. See if it's near failure. See if there's a conversation worth having. You'd need to know what your techs out in the fields are saying but also not saying, so that day in the life may also need to include ride-alongs.

Your wheels will begin to turn. You'll notice what they're trained for and not trained for, what they're incentivized to do and also not. Quite often, they aren't trained for it *and* aren't incentivized for it. They don't get any more money if they notice a failing water heater and create a future job, for example, and I'm talking about a lot more than water heaters here.

Perhaps you also, during these first couple of weeks, realize the previous owner didn't really track any of those, any of who is doing what and who isn't. So you have a business where revenue had been capped, and not because demand wasn't there but because the last owner didn't know how to capture it.

That's a solvable problem. But you can't solve it until you see it. That's your first two or three weeks. Once you understand the day-to-day—and once you understand the sales process—the next question becomes, *What are the obstacles to growth?* Sometimes, there isn't some complicated obstacle; sometimes, the obstacle is the owner didn't care.

For example, as of this writing, I have just acquired another company. The company had been doing $2 million in revenue approximately every year for the last seven years with about $700,000 in EBITDA. There hadn't been growth because the guy hadn't really tried. He didn't want to take on new kinds of work, and he didn't want to hire the people it would take to do new kinds of work. I learned from a key employee that he'd say something like, "In order to do that I'd have to hire someone and that would cost me $120,000 a year. I don't want to do that." But by hiring that $120,000 person, he might have been able to take on $1 million in additional work.

When I bought the commercial electrical contractor, their best year ever was $12 million. I made the decision that we would be hiring more people, buying new equipment, and altering compensation plans to incentivize technicians and support personnel to become salespeople. We just did $15 million and are already on track to crest over $20 million this coming year. Now, this wasn't because I discovered some secret totally hidden from the previous owner. It was because I decided I don't care if it takes three months of training before someone is profitable. I'm willing to take less money personally in distributions in order to make the business bigger. So part of your job this first month is identifying what the obstacle to growth really is.

THE FIRST SIX MONTHS AND BEYOND

Once you identify the growth obstacles, and assuming no crisis wipes the business out in the first month, you are going to begin implementing the changes you see that are needed—and you will track whether it works (or not) and how well (or not). Maybe it will take you more than six months to figure it out. Fine. It's not fair to say, "We could have done this the whole year." You didn't know yet. But once you implement it—month six, month eight, month ten—are the numbers starting to move? That's what matters. (Along the way, I highly, highly, **highly** recommend you create a business operations manual.)

For now, once you've made it through those first thirty days without anything breaking, now you're ready for the next stage—the longer transition realities, the handoff structures, and the longer learning curves that come after the sale.

CHAPTER 12

How to Work *in* Your Business (and *on* It)

THE BUSINESS IS YOURS. NOTHING CATASTROPHIC has happened. Nothing is broken (too badly). You're still here. Good.

So, we've covered the immediate aftermath of the sale—your first couple of days, your first couple of weeks, and roughly your first one to six months at a high level. Now we zoom in. You work both inside the business and on it, a technician-manager-operator, to paraphrase Michael Gerber. The questions get more specific yet, paradoxically, more general. For example, you'll be asking yourself such questions, *What exactly do **I** do here?*

We do not want you to have just bought yourself a full-time job with a lifestyle paycheck, but an actual asset. So, the advice herein is going to help you slowly-but-surely extricate yourself from your business so that within a reasonable amount of time, your business truly runs without you. That's the dream; let's make it real.

All that laid out, here's a few things that are likely true right about now in the business ownership journey, from the date of the sale into the first days and weeks and months.

- You may still have the previous owner involved, perhaps as an actual hire or on an earn-out timeline.
  - The latter is more likely.
  - If not the owner, then, like I did, maybe you made a key employee your partner.
- You're learning the industry in a much deeper way than you understood it in due diligence, and that's even if you previously knew this space from before all this started.
- You might be discovering that people have jobs but not really roles . . . or responsibilities but not really accountability . . . or loyalty to the old owner but not yet to you (we'll fix that, stat).
- And finally, likeliest of all, you're now realizing that if you keep doing everything the way the old owner did it, the company will never scale, and all you will ever own is a glorified job.

Any of these—all of them, really—is normal. Also typical is the systematic process to solve for them all. So as we begin the end of this book, we're going to cover the necessaries of this fresh-hot stage of business ownership. And it starts with . . .

FIGURING OUT WHAT THE PREVIOUS OWNER ACTUALLY DID

> Didn't we talk about your first few days at the company already? In the last chapter?

Sort of. The earliest hours of transitions, your eyes should be all over the company. You're watching how this thing actually works. You're taking notes, logging dependencies and bottlenecks and the like, and overall, you're ensuring nothing goes irreparably wrong.

Now, a few weeks in, you can finally focus. Zoom in on **three categories** of work the previous owner had been doing so you can (a) do his job well and then (b) make the job mostly redundant—or systematized so you can promote, delegate, or hire (we'll talk about that a little, too).

The first category is **financial oversight and management**. We talked about account transfer in the last oversight. This is more involved. The previous owner was probably the one paying himself, which meant he was also probably the one who knew how money actually moved through the company. He may have handled invoicing, collections, bill pay, and vendor priority. He also probably had experience with which customers pay slowly, where the pinch points were, and what had to get delayed when cash got tight. After learning how, exactly, this company works from the inside, go all-in with finances. Take that off his plate, if he's still at the company, briefly or for the medium term at minimum. Regardless, the old owner will not have sufficiently transitioned out while remaining the old financial nerve center of your new business.

The second category is **customer- and vendor-facing work**. If the company is consumer-facing, the owner may not be heavily involved in every customer interaction—or, he may be way too involved. In an ideal retail or home-service business, the owner is not answering the phone, quoting every call, and handling every upset customer. You should have someone answering calls, someone scheduling, a system for routing to service technicians, and some kind of CRM or workflow that doesn't depend on one person remembering everything.

But a lot of boomer-owned businesses don't work that way.

The owner still fields service calls. He still sends quotes himself. He still answers the email. He still knows where every lead came from because the business is basically his personal nervous system. If that's the case, you need to understand something very clearly: ***You will never scale if you keep doing that.***

If the owner is still fielding customer calls and generating quotes and sending them himself, and you don't replace that, then eventually that person becomes you. If your goal is to own and oversee the business rather than operate it every day forever, you have to replace that dependency. That means setting up the things a real business needs, like call intake, CRM, scheduling, dispatch, documented workflows, clear escalation paths, and actual systems. It may not all happen at once. But if you don't build it, the company will stay trapped at the level of one owner's personal bandwidth.

If yours is a B2B business, this is probably all the previous owner did all workday. In commercial companies, for example, the owner manages relationships with the big general contractors. He may be the one making deals, negotiating prices, smoothing over problems, getting invited to lunch, getting called first, or beating up vendors on price. If that's (still) the case with your company and the previous owner, you don't rip that away from him on day one. Not even day ninety, if you can help it by then. Rather, you let the last guy stay the lead while you shadow, listen, introduce yourself, collect contact information, take key client contacts to lunch, and begin developing your own relationships alongside his. The previous owner is still the lead for a while, but you are slowly becoming familiar enough that when he says in front of a client, referring to you, "OK , I'm going to let you take this one," the people on the other side already know you, trust you, and feel like they're dealing with basically a business owner.

The ideal is that after a few months, the previous owner is basically saying, "Work with him. He speaks for me. You have my cell phone if you need me, but he's handling this."

And by the time people realize he's barely around anymore, they don't care because they're already comfortable with you. Do they need to know that the old guy sold the business over to you weeks or months ago? They do not!

On to the third category, **employee management**. In a very small business, say below $3 million a year in top line revenue, the owner is directly managing everyone. In a somewhat larger one, he may be managing three or four key people who then manage everyone else. If you have foremen or supervisors, he may be managing them, and they're managing their crews. All this management going on . . .

Now, see, this is where many small business owners are weak—they usually don't have real career discussions with any of their underlings about what comes next for them. They don't have formal performance reviews. They don't have promotion tracks. Many employees in small to midsize companies, even if we're talking up to eight figures in annual revenue, they only get one kind of feedback from the owner—they get yelled at when something goes wrong. Emotional overcorrection is not management.

So, if you want more out of the business than the old owner got, you're going to have to learn those three categories of his job. Then do better than he did; you have the energy, and the motivation. You even have him there alongside you, most likely for at least a little while, to receive relevant advice from. That said . . .

Get the Previous Owner Out As Soon As Possible (Just Not Too Soon)

There's a reason almost everyone who has done this gives the same advice: ***Get the previous owner out as quickly as you reasonably can.*** There may be no reason to doubt the guy's integrity. You may even like him. But if he stays on too long, conflict becomes inevitable. Why? Well, isn't it obvious? You cannot have two bosses in one room forever. Have you ever heard of a company with two CEOs? What are they, co-CEOs? That would be like . . . two husbands in a marriage!

I'll stop.

Back to business. Allowing the previous owner to take his leave is something you want, but perhaps not right away. If the former owner has an earn-out, the ideal situation is that you are paying him to do almost nothing. That sounds wasteful until you understand what it means. If the business hits the agreed-upon EBITDA or performance metrics over the next couple years, he gets paid. He is still obligated to help if you need him to. But your goal should be to reach a point where you can hit those targets without needing him day to day. That's a win, see? He gets a fair price for the business. You get the benefit of the transition and the confidence that he's still there if you absolutely need him. But practically, he becomes a backup, not an operator. That's what you want. And you may want him around (until you don't).

As I've implied, if the business depends heavily on his relationships—especially long-time, high-paying client relationships—you cannot usually get him out immediately. You need some period of transition because if you make that transition too sudden, you risk losing personal goodwill. In most cases, you want the actual period of active involvement to be much shorter than what the contract technically allows. My transition plan with the previous owner of what's now my electrical contracting firm was one year. Now, that was the plan; he was out within three weeks. I realized I could replace the three things he was doing. He wasn't doing all three in a heavy way, and once I saw what was real and what wasn't, I could get those pieces off his plate quickly. So yes, the contract said one thing. Reality made it a lot shorter. How did I pull that off? What were those three categories again? Three weeks, was it? Putting it all together now?

Very good. But to make sure the wrong kind of sparks don't fly, we've got to cover the psychological component of old owner, new owner interaction.

Don't Treat the Previous Owner Like a Previous Owner

Tread carefully; do not frame your relationship as, *I'm the boss now, and here's what I need you to do.* That will create friction faster than almost anything else. Instead, phrase everything as if he is helping you. Which, in a sense, he is. Ask him for help. I'm being lateral.

- "I'm trying to understand this."
- "Can you help me think through this?"
- "I really want to do a good job with this customer."
- "This employee's doing X; I need him doing Y. What do you think?"

You are still directing the ship, but psychologically, you are allowing the previous owner to feel useful rather than diminished. It won't work forever, but it will work for a while.

And then, at some point, you will need to move the company far enough away from the way he did it that he either can't help or doesn't want to. That's normal, and that's why you want to move him out as quickly as you can once the handoff is secure.

Performance: Goals, Measurement, Incentives

The third category of the owner's work that you'll be taking over is employee management. Briefly touched on earlier, it's got to get covered in full. Remember that operations manual you begin building in the last chapter through those day-in-the-life interviews? It's about to come back up all over again.

Now, it's neat to have a map of operations. But the real value at this stage of a manual with processes and procedures documented is you get a stark view of what employees are doing . . . what they are actually doing . . . versus what all they should be doing.

When inexperienced entrepreneurs in my network ask me how to create performance standards, quarterly review agenda, promotion paths, and all the rest that a big company offers employees to coax them to stay, I tell them they're starting with the wrong deliverables. See, they're basically thinking in as many words, *What should I tell this employee to be doing?* That's too low-level. Rather, not low enough. I'm talking profit margins here. And then some. Let me ask you: Where do you want this business to be in six months, twelve months, eighteen months? It's a catch-all question. It can cover:

- top-line revenue
- gross profit
- net income
- back-office overhead
- customer satisfaction
- retention
- lead flow
- conversion
- average ticket
- margin by job type
- whatever else matters in your industry/business

Is this obvious? Yes. But also, no. Not really. A shocking number of small business owners do not track the things they think they understand. For example, I know an entrepreneur whose business offers underground digging for commercial electrical. He also does hardscape landscaping because the same excavator operators can work in both businesses. Fine. But he doesn't actually know what he makes money on because he isn't tracking it that way. He knows the money coming in, and he knows total payroll. He does not know how many hours a particular person spent digging versus landscaping versus something else. He does not know the gross profit by job type. He only knows high-level money in, money out. That is not enough. You need to know the numbers in a way that lets you act.

So first, define the goals. What numbers do you want to see? Make sure you can actually measure the numbers that tell you whether you're reaching them. Often, that means building the tracking system almost entirely from scratch. For example, you may need people to input hours differently. You may need purchases assigned to jobs. You may need costs categorized correctly. You may need sixty days or more just to get enough clean data to be worth analyzing. That's fine. You're not going to know everything on day one. But if you don't start measuring, you will never know what levers to pull.

How KPIs Drive Employee Performance

Once you know the goals and once you're measuring the right things to milestone your way there, now you can ask the next useful question: ***What levers do I have to pull to get from here to there?***

Maybe the problem is marketing spend. Or lead conversion. Maybe the problem is your employees are good at selling but you don't get enough leads. We sort of touched on this in the previous chapter. It comes up again because it can't go away. Or maybe the problem is that you get plenty of leads but your people don't upsell. Or the problem is that you're pushing lower-margin products instead of higher-margin ones. Or that you don't know which product categories are actually producing your margin. Or all of these. Maybe none at all. Until you measure the flow—leads, conversions, products purchased, margin by product or job type, cost by project—you won't know. And if you don't know, you can't build a sensible key performance indicator (KPI) structure, which is how you restructure employee compensation to incentivize them to take your company where you want it to go. See? The goals you set become the KPIs you decide, then those become employee incentives, which then become goals achieved.

Performance Review: A Path, Not a Threat

One of the best things you can do as a new owner is give your employees something they've probably never had before—a career plan. Most SMB employees are used to one of two things: either being ignored, or, like I said earlier, just being yelled at. They are not used to someone saying anything like the following:

- "I want you to be in this position."
- "I want you making this greater percentage than you do now."
- "Here's how you get there."
- "Here's what we're measuring."
- "Here's where you are."
- "Here's how your bonus works."
- "Here's what the guy doing better than you is doing differently."

The way to make change tolerable is to make it beneficial. No one likes change in the abstract. But if they can see that the change means more money, better work, a more stable company, and a clear path for them, they will tolerate a lot more than you think. That said, it can feel awkward at first. *What's the new guy's real agenda?* But I'm telling you . . . if you follow through—if the bonus is real, the pay bump is real, the promotion is real—they get excited about it very quickly.

My electrical contracting company never had performance reviews before. Bonuses were basically Christmas bonuses, which were whatever the owner felt like giving that year. Now we do performance reviews twice a year, and we tie bonuses to actual performance. We tell guys, *If you had done this and this, your bonus would have been this. You didn't, so it's this.* Then in the next cycle, some of them actually improve. Now they get the bigger bonus. Better behavior, better morale, better company.

A good example is upsell in a service business. Say you want your HVAC guys, while they're out on an HVAC service call, to also check the water heater and mention it if it's old and likely to need replacement. That may not be something they've ever thought to do. You care about it because you want your service people to also be salespeople when the situation calls for it.

So now you coach them. You give them the script. Explain the expectation. Measure it. Commission it. Review it. It's not yet more work for no reward. Absolutely not. It's a little extra effort for a lot more upside. If you can connect company success to employee success, the whole thing changes. Now it's not, "*The new owner is making my life harder.*" It's, "*The new owner is making this feel like a real company, and I can make more money here.*"

By the way, while we're on the subject of raising employee's expectations of themselves, I'd be remiss to forget about this common skill issue—relationships as essential to the job. This is not just for salespeople. If your project managers or supervisors need to be strong with general contractors, pre-construction managers, or key customer contacts—for example—then relationship-building is part of the job. You need to make that explicit.

I tell my people, *I need you to take them to dinner, take them to a concert, take them shooting, take them to lunch. I don't care. Just get to know them.* Because if the business grows, it cannot just be me and my business partner who knows everyone. People move. PMs get replaced. New people come in. If all the relationships sit at the top, we've created another bottleneck. We don't want that. So we make the opposite, part of the performance review. For every key GC, I tell them I want them to have taken out a PM at least once a quarter. They've got to write it all down, too.

- Who did you take out?
- Where did you go?
- What's their role?
- What's their personality?
- What did you learn?

That is part of the job. And if you do it, guess what? Your bonus is bigger.

Scaling With Specialists

This is a more advanced management and ownership subject, but I perceive that by now, you're ready. And it goes like this . . .

At a certain point, you need to stop relying on jacks of all trades for critical roles. Generalists can keep things moving. Specialists let you grow without constant hidden errors. A perfect example is a controller. I was convinced a couple months in that we needed a full-time controller at my contracting company. Someone who understood construction accounting but the in's and out's for my specific electrical niche. Someone who could handle the books, enter invoices correctly, follow up with PMs, make sure costs were categorized properly, and make it so that at any given point I could run a report and trust that it was right.

My partner did not want to spend the money. From his perspective, a good controller was expensive—$120,000 plus bonuses and benefits. He came from an owner who never wanted to hire anyone expensive, because the owner wasn't trying to grow and didn't care about building a real machine.

I knew we needed her. I knew that, generally speaking, if you don't hire the right specialist for a key function, you end up three years later realizing you should have done it, after three years of struggle, bad data, and heartburn.

So we hired her. At first, my partner was frustrated. She didn't know every intricacy of electrical immediately. Fine. That's normal.

A couple months later, he was singing her praises. She was catching mistakes in real time. For example, a PM would say, "Put $20,000 on this job and $10,000 on this one." And she would come back and ask, "OK, but what does that mean? Is that cost? Is that revenue? Is profit in there? What markup are we charging? What exactly is the customer being billed?"

Without her, that would have gone through wrong. In one case, that kind of mistake would have cost us almost $10,000. One mistake. If she finds ten of those in a year, she has paid for herself.

Even beyond the money, the value is that I know the numbers are right. I don't have to discover six months later that something has been miscategorized for half a year and spend a week digging through books trying to figure out what happened.

Specialists prevent pain; they also free your best people to do what only they can do. For example, my partner shouldn't be entering things into QuickBooks. He should be managing PMs, supervisors, customers, and jobs. That is what he uniquely does well. The controller handles what she uniquely does well. That is how the company gets stronger. Specializing means scaling.

And speaking of a partner, you might have one in this venture, too. A quick note on that: If you have a COO, president, minority owner, or key operator who is both employee and partner, then you need a real relationship with them. Obviously. But I'll explain. In my case, my partner is a minority owner—he's both the president and the COO. He's my employee in one sense, but he's also my partner. And ideally, if you structure it right, your incentives are aligned. His salary is fair. His equity grows if the company grows. Dividends matter to him. The company winning matters to him.

So you should not be arguing over the goals. If there is disagreement, it should be about how to get there. If you've done that right, that's healthy.

Big picture, there are going to be areas where you defer to him because he knows the business and the industry better than you do. And there are going to be areas where he needs to defer to you, because your background gives you better instincts there.

That was the controller issue. He knew commercial electrical better than I did; I knew the value of a specialist better than he did. So I told him plainly, *I need you to trust me on this*. And then you have to be right. I was. And if you're not, you need to admit it and fix it to get the right thing done. Because the more often you're right, the more trust builds. The more he will defer to you in the areas where you're strong, just as you should defer to him where he's strong. That's what a real operating partnership looks like.

INTERMEDIATE TO ADVANCED INDUSTRY KNOWHOW TO KNOW

Once the people side starts taking shape, you run into the next layer of learning—the business-specific mechanics. And at the top of that list is this: ***How do you pay, and how do you get paid?*** That is one of the fastest ways to go bankrupt even when the business is "profitable." Take commercial electrical. I might be net-30 with my vendors. I buy a generator today, and I have to pay for it within thirty days. But I may not bill my customer for that until later in the month, and even then the customer may be net-60. So the actual cash may not show up until day seventy-five or later. So even if I have the receivable, I don't have the cash. Payroll does not care that you have receivables; payroll cares whether the bank account clears.

Then add retainage. In my business, 10 percent of the contract gets held back until the entire project finishes. That means I might have hundreds of thousands of dollars—sometimes mostly profit—sitting out there waiting to come in months later. That's normal in this line of work. But if you don't understand that rhythm, you panic or mismanage cash.

If you're running a retail or service business where customers swipe a card onsite, you have a completely different cash rhythm. So this is very industry- and business-specific. You have to learn it.

Then there's customer acquisition. For example, do you know what's baseline-typical for . . .

- walk-ins?
- online leads?
- referrals?
- existing relationships?
- repeat business?
- commercial bids?
- **reputation?**

I've bolded that last bullet because it's a bit more complex than some of the others, as it's largely perception-based. In B2B, reputation is more so informal feedback and relationship quality. In B2C, it's Google reviews, online surveys, and repeat calls.

Then come **licenses** and **regulations**. Do you know about these?

Who needs to have them renewed, by when, and how much? Closely related to this industry-specific issue is **seasonality**. If you're HVAC, the details vary by geography. If you're roofing, maybe winter is different. If you have guys on roofs, maybe there are ancillary services you can offer in a slow season, e.g., Christmas lights, gutter work, whatever fits.

Then there is one of the most complex issues in all of business—**margin maintenance**. I've saved the best for last, just for you.

In most industries, you can grow by taking on a bunch of lower-margin work. Fine. You can also turn that down and chase only very high-margin work. Fine. Both strategies have risk. If you take too much lower-margin work, you're busy but not creating the kind of profit you want. If you rely only on higher-margin work, you may end up with people sitting around waiting for those jobs to materialize. If they don't, you're bleeding payroll.

So what we realized in electrical contracting was we needed anchor jobs—large jobs with decent profit that keep a significant portion of our workforce busy profitably. Then we reserve part of the workforce to chase really high-margin work. That lets us do both, granting us base stability but also immense upside opportunity.

That was not something the old owner had really spent much time thinking about. He had been coasting. He was happy with what he was making. Growth was not the priority. That is often the opportunity for you as the buyer. Just the willingness to think strategically about a business the old owner had stopped trying to optimize . . . that alone creates some magic.

FROM FEW TO MORE TO FEWER

At every point in this stage, you are the owner, even if during the first weeks and months you're doing more working *in* than *on*. Your job is to set the goals, measure the goals, incentivize the people, and then knock out the obstacles that prevent the business from reaching those goals. At first, that feels like a lot. It is a lot. Yeah, I know. But, if you do it right, you don't have to keep rebuilding the company from scratch every year.

Once you've set up the measurements, you don't need to reinvent them. Once you've set up the role clarity, you don't need to recreate it. Once you've set up the incentive structure, you may tweak it, but you don't have to start over. And once you've hired the right specialist, you don't need to do their job forever. That means over time, if you're doing it correctly, there is less and less for you to do personally.

You may still decide on goals, adjust incentives, approve a marketing budget increase, and still spend a month interviewing for a key hire (as another example). But that's not forty hours a week forever; that's owner work. And the real question becomes the same one you asked about the previous owner: ***What do I need to take off my plate so that I don't need to spend ten hours a week on this anymore?***

If you've done this correctly, you are gradually getting rid of your own job. You've built systems, hired people, measured correctly, and aligned incentives well enough that the business can run without your hands on every switch.

You do not want to reinvent the wheel every month. You want to do it correctly once, then tweak. And that is how you move from owner-operator to owner-overseer. You no longer work for your business; it works for you.

You made it.

CHAPTER 13

Legacy (and What All This Was For)

BY THIS POINT, YOU HAVE THE FULL PLAN. YOU know what kind of business you're probably going to buy. You know how to find it, whether on-market or off-market. You know how to win the favor of the owner so you can be the one who buys it. You know how to properly vet a deal so you can confirm it's what it needs to be and not some scam; you know how to know what you're getting into. And if you follow this full process—without deviating even a half-step—what you should end up with is something your current (or former) career no longer allows you to build in this economy—**real wealth**.

Small business entrepreneurship-by-acquisition is the alternative career path. You're not the only beneficiary; you're basically Baby Boomer business salvation, coming to this generation's rescue to preserve their life's work for the next generation. This, I believe, is the best way to earn a living for most of you reading this.

But that raises a bigger question: *Why?*

More specifically . . . what's the purpose of all this? What's the purpose of entrepreneurship? The purpose of wealth creation?

Of work itself? If the answers are all just about making more money, then we've missed the point.

See, work is *not* a necessary evil. And now I find myself feeling frustrated over so much modern Christian church-culture teaching about work. *Work so we can provide. Work so we can pay the mortgage and feed the kids. Work is a duty and a toil. Work for years so one day you can retire and never work again.*

Re-think that. They're telling us the purpose of something is to be able to one day stop doing it? Excuse me?

OK, sure. Yes. Paying your mortgage. Good. Taking care of your kids. Good. Leisure time. Good, too. But have a pass at Genesis, and you'll notice that the first thing God does after creating Adam and Eve is give an assignment. Some work. Literally a job. Several, actually. Specifically? Three:

1. Name all the animals.
2. Subdue the earth.
3. Have lots of sex (not kidding; Genesis 1:28, 9:1, and 9:7).

Some entries on that list to me seem more like work than others. Our point is not the what but the why. Many modern employed professionals—even a staggering number of Christians I know—speak and act as if work only exists because of the Fall, when sin entered the world. Because work itself is a punishment. As if the ideal human life is one in which you avoid work altogether. That's not what Genesis says. Before the Fall, there was work. We are made to work.

Now, the work we do is not just a means to a paycheck; it is in and of itself . . . *good.* It's good for the world, and it's good for us.

And especially for men, there is something deeply important about being able to say with honorable pride, "I did something today. I accomplished something."

That's one of the things that frustrates me so much about the global AI conversation and its tag-team idea, universal basic income, which are together alleged to one day solve all financial problems. Look, you can give people money all day long, but if they're just sitting around, if they're not accomplishing anything, that's no solution. That's a good way to create a bunch of disaffected young men. There is nothing more dangerous than a bunch of disaffected young men.

So, one of the reasons I wrote this book is to show you this alternative career path as more than a way to make money; it's, in my view, the best way to do something meaningful—for yourself, your family, and for the world. Owning your own business puts the weight on you. No one is going to hand you anything. If it succeeds, if it grows, if it creates wealth, it will be because *you* did something that was **yours**. Revelations 21 describes the nations of the earth bringing their glories to place it before God. That's what you just added to. You used your talent, your hard work, and built something good that you will present to God Himself. It's not a necessary evil.

That is good for people. That is good for men. That is good for our families. That is what God Himself requires of us.

That said, I believe both within the church and without, we get wealth-building wrong. We deem it inherently suspect somehow. *Oh, you want to get rich? So you want to lie, cheat, scam, and steal, do you?* Highly suspect. Sometimes, you'll hear religious commentary spun into this view, with wealth described as worldly, morally compromising, or obviously unbiblical. Again, suspect. To paraphrase King Solomon, a wise man leaves an inheritance for his children and his children's children. Where's the condemnation of wealth? Nope, that's a mandate for stewardship. You should want to build something that outlasts you. You should want to build something your children and your children's children can benefit from. And yet that's exactly what the modern wage economy steals from us . . . speaking of theft!

If you live entirely on salary, maybe with a 401(k), then what are you really leaving? You can't pass your résumé down to your kids. You can't leave your performance reviews to your grandchildren. You can't pass your promotions, your corporate relationships, or the conditions of the economy that kept you employed down to anyone either. All die or retire with you, whichever comes first.

But—suppose you build and oversee a sound, profitable business—if you put the right people in place, the right systems in place, the right goals in place—then now you own something that can outlast you. Not just with money but with purpose.

Speaking for me, I hope my kids inherit my businesses. I can't gift them my corporate job in a trust, but I can teach them how to run Dad's business. So, I can leave them a business if they want it. Then they can build on it; maybe they can leave it to their children, my grand-children, and then, them, to theirs, too. And so on.

That is legacy. It used to be normal. So normal that's where many surnames came from; my last name is *Parker* because we guarded the parks for the nobles of England. Most Western-world names are tied to roles, to continuity of those roles, as they passed down through the centuries and beyond. We've lost that. All of it. We are so transitory now—where we live, what we do, how we think about work, what we believe our obligations are. Because of that, we are rootless.

Small business acquisition allows you to opt out of salary-seeking behaviors and opt into the good, transcendent life of asset ownership. I'm going to build something that stays. That stays and protects.

Especially for men, this is key. The male soul craves freedom and meaning above all. In this case, freedom means not being a wage slave to people who hate you. And yes, I mean hate and you. Both, specifically.

If you're a straight white Christian man, there are would-be saboteurs crawling all over and inside and on top of and around the modern corporate world. They hiss at your very existence. Because they hate you; they see you as both their prey and their predator, paradoxically. If they ever hire you, it's often because they have to; the only qualified, competent candidates belong to this most-hated demographic set. They'll make up for it though, by failing to compensate and otherwise reward you as you are owed. You may have to be better than everyone else just to be treated as equal. You will sit through humiliating seminars. You will swallow things you should not have to swallow. And at the first opportunity, you are very likely to be first on the chopping block—even if you are directly responsible for immense amounts of revenue generation.

Don't put your future—or your kids' future—in the hands of people who hate you.

The big institutions are easy for these people to control because they are centralized. If you take over some giant corporation, you control thousands and thousands of people at once. That's attractive—to them.

American small business is different. In the SMB space—in construction, home services, gray-collar and blue-collar work—you generally do not find anti-Christians. The kind of person who wants to do this sort of work is not usually the same person who majored in theater at Brown University and wants to turn the workplace into an ideological training ground for literally Communism.

Because of that, you have more control. You are doing work they do not want to do, and they will never want to do it. But the work is still needed. That's the beautiful part; it's needed more than just about all else. We could probably eliminate 60, 70, maybe 80 percent of all corporate jobs and the world would mostly keep going. Twitter already proved that. Elon Musk fired huge portions of the company, and it still functioned, even better in many ways. A lot of corporate jobs are basically useless, and with AI, that is only going to become more obvious. That is not true for electricians. It's not true for plumbers. And it's not true for roofers, HVAC technicians, drain cleaners, or any of the other tradesmen and service professionals who keep real life moving.

When the AC dies, nobody cares that you are a straight white Christian male. They need it fixed. When the roof leaks, nobody cares what you believe. They need it fixed. When the pipes burst, nobody cares how conservative or "based" your politics are. They need it fixed. And if they need it fixed, they will pay you for it. So, in a very real sense, you are taking control back from the very people who hate you—*and they are paying you now*.

That's freedom.

I Have Something For You

If you've made it this far, don't just close the book and think, *That was interesting.* Take the next step; go get the freebies. My **Letter Of Intent** and **Purchase Agreement** templates are yours free at:

bluebacks.co/downloads

And if you're super-serious about small business entrepreneurship—perhaps you have a deal in front of you or you think you may soon—**buy some of my time**. I help people vet deals. I help would-be buyers think through whether the thing they're looking at is real, whether the structure makes sense, whether the risks are manageable, and whether there is a way to make the deal work intelligently. And in the right situation, I may even come in as an investor or partner with you. Certainly not for everyone, but there will be some deals that are worth doing together.

Book a few minutes with me today at:

bluebacks.co/schedule

One more thing. If you're part of a faith-based organization—a church, a faith-and-works nonprofit, a private school, or anything like that—please consider bringing me in to speak to your students, to your people. As I've made clear, I believe that one of the deepest failures of our current moment is that we have lied to young Christians, especially young men, about work, about entrepreneurship, about wealth, about vocation, and about what freedom really requires. I want to help fix that. I want to show them a path that is real, honorable, productive, wealth-building, and rooted in Christian duty. That is legacy. That is freedom.

And together, we can bring it to the next generation.

One way or another, I hope to hear from you soon.

Thank you for reading, and God bless.

ACKNOWLEDGMENTS

To my family, for believing in me.

To my business partner, Landon, the best bet I ever made.

To my college buddy and fellow Christian Bayard, who if you have a good business and need capital, he's your guy.

To the professionals I met along the way who helped me vet things and made it happen: Alan, Rich, and Terry.

Thank you all!

ABOUT THE AUTHOR

Wayne "Tripp" Parker III triple-majored at Duke University in computer science, electrical and computer engineering, and philosophy. A native of small-town North Carolina, Tripp moved to Seattle after graduation where he worked in fintech, healthtech, and early AI and machine learning in the wearables space. As he watched the technologies he helped build begin to automate away aspects of his own job, he grew increasingly disillusioned. Compounded by a cultural mismatch with DEI policies that punished excellence and rewarded incompetence, he decided it was time to leave tech—but go where? Drawing on his experience in predictive product design from R&D, Tripp repurposed his education and skill set to take a new path—commercial electrical contracting entrepreneurship through acquisition. He now owns two companies and enjoys a mid-eight-figure net worth at age forty-one. Today, he teaches business professionals how to secure their own financial future by sourcing, purchasing, and managing undervalued blue-collar or gray-collar small businesses—ones offering products and services that are difficult or impossible to automate with current and near-future technology.

www.ingramcontent.com/pod-product-compliance
Lightning Source LLC
LaVergne TN
LVHW090348240926
848801LV00017B/182/J
* 9 7 9 8 9 9 6 4 8 2 9 0 0 *